A Strange Elation

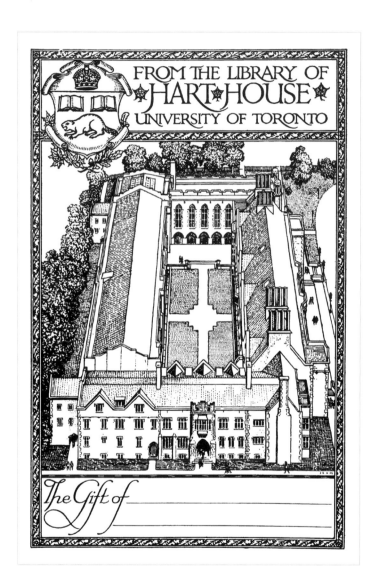

FROM THE LIBRARY OF
HART HOUSE
UNIVERSITY OF TORONTO

The Gift of _____
_____

A Strange Elation

Hart House: The First Eighty Years

Published by Hart House

Printed and bound by University of Toronto Press

Editor: David Kilgour

Design by Bruce Mau Design
Bruce Mau with Chris Pommer and Chris Rowat.

Typeset by Richard Hunt

Canadian Cataloguing in Publication Data

Main entry under title:
A strange elation: Hart House, the first eighty years

Includes index.
ISBN 0-7727-0647-6 (bound)
ISBN 0-7727-0649-2 (pbk.)

1. Hart House – History. 1. Kilgour, David. 11. Hart House

LE3.T538H35   378.713'541   C99-9322151-X

Contents

There in the quiet library, with the sunlight glinting on the red sofa and the natural wood panelling, all was bathed in a soft glow, and it became a world in which he experienced a strange elation...

Morley Callaghan
The Varsity Story, 1948

Introduction

As warden of Hart House, I'm a relative newcomer, and still capable of being amazed and enchanted by the variety of events and activities that take place within its walls. One recent morning I looked at the list of the day's meetings posted behind the Porters' Desk and was amazed yet again. At 8:00 A.M., a working group was meeting to develop campus educational initiatives regarding homelessness. Later in the morning, Hindu, Tamil, and African students' groups would hold meetings. Several faith communities were gathering for spiritual observances. In the afternoon, SAC (Students' Administrative Council) was conducting a workshop on student debt and youth unemployment. In the evening, there was a wealth of cultural events including an orchestra rehearsal, Camera Club activities, and a Film Board screening.

But the list of meetings represented only a fraction of what the day would bring. As usual, the doors had opened for athletics users at 6:45 A.M., and, also as usual, there had been a line-up. The Arbor Room was open for breakfast. Soon students would drift upstairs to read (or snooze) in the Library, or study in one of the common rooms. Occasionally the sound of a piano or violin would echo in the halls. The art gallery would open, and then the Gallery Grill, where many alumni come for lunch.

And all day long, of course, small, unrecorded personal dramas would unfold — conversations intense, sublime or ridiculous; relationships beginning with a glance in the Arbor Room; unexpected reunions in the halls. Only when the doors closed at midnight would a hush fall over the building.

How can a single book document the history of a place that has touched and continues to touch the lives, hearts, and souls of hundreds of thousands of people? When we got the idea for a volume to celebrate the House's eightieth anniversary on the eve of the millennium, we did what comes naturally to everyone here: we set up a committee. (Hart House is, in fact, run by student-led committees, from the Board of Stewards on down. The amazing thing is that they work—most of the time.)

We quickly agreed that a dry, linear history of the House was not what we wanted. We also agreed that no one book could cover every aspect of life here; we would have to sacrifice, for instance, the biannual Finnish Exchange, the chess and bridge clubs, and a whole catalogue of activities, events, groups, and people too numerous to even begin to list here.

One objective we all agreed on: we wanted the book to reflect the many voices and many lives of Hart House, often crossing, often chaotic, always evolving.

In the end, we asked various authors to write chapters about subjects that were of primary importance, from the founding principles of the House to the current day. We commissioned photographer Steven Evans to create a portfolio of timeless images of the building. And we solicited members of the public, both well known and unknown, to contribute their own memories and reflections.

The result, we feel, is a book that is true to its subject: inclusive, lively, anecdotal, sometimes raucous and even discordant.

It would have been easy to write an elegiac account of the House, but that would suggest that the "great days" are over—and of course they are not. Hart House once represented the best of art, music, literature, theatre, and athletics in Toronto. Now—thanks in part to the fact that many of its members went on to establish new theatre groups, musical ensembles, and artists' and writers' collectives—it is only one of many cultural centres in the city. But it is as vibrant and creative as ever, and the story of its evolution is fascinating and important.

Who could have known that the original Founders' Prayer of the House would continue to be so profoundly relevant to student, faculty, staff, and alumni members in such a changed world eighty years later? Hart House was conceived for a campus of 3,500 students who were mostly white Anglo-Saxon men, but today the Founders' Prayer expresses the democratic social values of the House to a campus of more than 50,000 students, the majority of whom are women and/or people of colour. While originally intended "for the exclusive use of the male members of the University" with special space reserved for the Young Men's Christian Association, the founding principles of Hart House have proven to be elastic as well as solid, and the House has responded to the changing social context of Toronto by becoming more inclusive. Although we still struggle to divest ourselves of the ghosts of perceptions that Hart House is exclusively for a white male elite, women are full members (and in fact run both the staff and most of the committees), and the House is home to a spectrum of faith groups that include Christians, Hindus, Muslims, Wiccans, and Pagans.

The House is at the centre of a whirl of campus activities these days. Not only are more than thirty Hart House clubs and committees flourishing, but many campus groups are now using the resources of the House too. The original democratic student-run structure for governance continues to adapt itself as new circumstances arise, requiring new policies. In addition to the student secretaries elected by the standing committees of the House and the presidential and governing council appointees, we now have representatives on the Board of Stewards from the three student governments (Students' Administrative Council, Graduate Students'

Union, and the Association of Part-Time Undergraduate Students) and from the campuses in Mississauga and Scarborough. Student secretaries gain invaluable first-hand experience as stewards of a multi-million-dollar organization charged with the keeping of a historic building and serving a campus constituency that is now the size of a small city.

Eighty percent of the students at the University of Toronto are from the Greater Toronto Area; they spend up to two hours each day commuting. Many work part-time to pay for their education, so they have little time left for co-curricular activities; but somehow they still give their time to be part of the enthusiastic student leadership at Hart House. I have had the privilege of attending Board of Stewards meetings where the quality of debate among the student stewards on difficult issues reflected such wisdom and thoughtful accountability that the chairperson and I had tears of pride in our eyes.

The building itself is organic and changing. Granted, there are drawbacks — we certainly wish, for instance, that the architects had included the elevator for which there seems to be a space behind the Porters' Desk. But the original rooms and halls still work beautifully for the myriad of activities, both organized and unorganized, which they frame. In fact, the very age of the building adds an element of wonder to everything we do within it. A permanent art gallery and a wheelchair access ramp have been added over the years, and we have even managed to wire the House unobtrusively for the computer network through the twelve-inch-thick brick walls. The heavy oak front doors are now opened with power assistance.

In the course of the next decade, we will be seeking to be more inclusive and relevant and engaged than ever in enhancing the life of the campus and the city. We will be reaching out to find and embrace students who are not currently using the House. As the suburban campuses grow, we will be finding ways to share the exhilaration of our activities with those students. In keeping with one of the original motivations for establishing Hart House — the belief that we should give all we can to make a difference in our society — we will be initiating campus-wide projects aimed at alleviating serious social problems such as homelessness. We will continue to find innovative ways to make the House universally accessible so that all students can benefit from the strange elation of the Hart House experience.

Margaret Hancock
Hart House
September 1999

The future site of Hart House, *c.*1870

4

Chapter 1
The Founder and the Animator

Ian Montagnes

Hart House was the creation of two young men. One conceived the plan and built the structure. The other breathed life into the fabric.

The first was a Canadian who loved things British, the second an Englishman who loved Canada. One moved on to a distinguished career as diplomat and statesman, eventually becoming the first Canadian-born governor general. The other refused all other careers once he arrived at Hart House, because to him no other work seemed as important.

The first was Vincent Massey. The second was Burgon Bickersteth. This is the story of how they created the institution — the living structure — we know as Hart House.

The process stretched over two decades, from 1910 to the mid-1920s. There was no master plan. The House evolved, adapting to meet needs, recognizing potential for growth, establishing standards, centring on education in its broadest sense.

Vincent Massey was in his fourth year at University College in 1910. The University of Toronto then was just emerging from a prolonged institutional adolescence. Recently freed from political interference by a new University Act, it had grown explosively in three years from about 2,500 students to nearly 4,000 (almost all men) — a handful by today's standards but a number that strained all the existing facilities. There were four arts colleges (University, Victoria, St. Michael's, and Trinity, the last of these still several kilometres to the southwest, on Queen Street) and five professional faculties (medicine and engineering, both long established, and three brand-new ones for forestry, education, and household science). The colleges and older faculties had come together in federation over several years, sometimes reluctantly. They had remained staunchly independent, in a relationship with the parent university not unlike that of feudal barons to their king.

View of the front hall of Hart House under construction

Students at the four arts colleges might be expected to meet, at least in passing, in classes. Otherwise few opportunities existed for them and students in the other faculties to come together as members of a single university. There were football games, more popular than they are today, and a few shared activities such as the production of *The Varsity*, but no residences for most of the men and only a few overcrowded centres for campus social life. These centres were, principally, a dining hall in University College, where the food was a source of constant complaint; a Students' Union in an old house on St. George Street, with billiard tables, common rooms, and a public telephone, which was open to all men students but could not accommodate even the 300 who belonged; an old red-brick gymnasium built for a much smaller university; and, finally, the Young Men's Christian Association, by all accounts the most vigorous organization of all. The Y had seven campus branches and, in addition to religious services and Bible classes, ran a housing registry, published student handbooks, and housed a small recreational centre.

Early in 1910 plans were announced for a campaign to build a large new headquarters for the YMCA. There was talk also of an expanded Students' Union. Vincent Massey's active participation in student life had made him familiar with the shortage of facilities. He foresaw, moreover, the danger of two competing centres, one for the YMCA, the other purely social. He discussed the matter with his father, Chester Massey. In February 1910 the elder Massey wrote to the chairman of the university's board of governors:

> On behalf of the Executors of the Estate of H.A. Massey I write to say that, if the project be considered favourably by the Board of Governors, they will be pleased to erect and equip a building for the University Young Men's Christian Association, also for the Students' Union, the two buildings to be connected by an Assembly Hall...
>
> It is the desire of the Executors to make this gift a memorial to my Father, the late Hart A. Massey.

So who was Hart Massey, a man whose first name by itself was enough to identify his memorial? He was, quite simply, the outstanding Canadian industrialist of his generation. From a small factory started by his father in Newcastle, Ontario, he had built the Massey-Harris Company into one of the world's largest manufacturers of farm implements and Canada's first major industrial exporter. Its bright red tractors and combines won prizes at international fairs in Europe and North America; they ploughed fields and harvested crops on most continents of the globe. At the end of the nineteenth century, the firm was one of Canada's largest employers. (Before the end of the twentieth, long separated from the Massey family, it had virtually disappeared.)

Hart Massey was tall and bearded, shrewd, stern, and austere. He was not well liked by Toronto's elite—a Methodist country boy, the grandson of immigrants from the United States, who had bought himself a mansion on Jarvis Street. He could be tough. It is said that one day, when he was touring the Massey-Harris plant, a workman, startled by the appearance of the boss, fell into a vat of vermilion paint; Massey watched the man emerge safely and then docked his pay for

Alice and Vincent Massey with children
on opening day, November 11, 1919

waste. But he was also a benevolent employer who believed in a responsibility beyond the exchange of money for labour. The Massey-Harris factory on King Street West in Toronto was a social centre. Its workers had their own mutual benefit society, library association, sports teams, auditorium, dramatic productions, band, string orchestra, and glee club.

Hart Massey believed in returning his wealth to the community, and gave generously during his lifetime to many causes. In Toronto, for example, he built Massey Hall, long the city's premier concert centre, and the Fred Victor Mission, which still provides assistance to the homeless and poor. When he died, in 1896, he left a will that was almost unprecedented in those days of light succession duties and inherited family firms. His family was provided for, but the bulk of his estate, including a controlling interest in Massey-Harris, was placed in trust to benefit carefully selected educational, religious, and public causes. The trustees were his three surviving children—Vincent Massey's father, uncle, and aunt. They treated the charge with care, giving the money to projects that had been planned to meet definite needs. One was Burwash Hall, a neo-Gothic dining hall and men's residence for Victoria College. Other donations went to churches and hospitals, to Toronto's musical life, and to the city's new museum and art gallery. Before he ever thought of Hart House, Vincent's aunt, Lillian Massey Treble, personally gave the money for, and helped plan, a home for the new Faculty of Household Science that included, as a gift to all the woman of the University of Toronto, an athletic section with a gymnasium and swimming pool. (Part of the building, on the southeast corner of Bloor Street and Avenue Road, has recently been converted into a Club Monaco clothing store.)

On his twenty-first birthday, Vincent Massey became a trustee of the Massey Estate. He was then an undergraduate. His family had for some time been looking for a suitable memorial to Hart Massey's public service. Given Vincent's background, it is not perhaps surprising that he should seize upon the opportunity to match a need of Canada's largest university with the desires of a family devoted to philanthropy. It took imagination to recognize that need, however, and even more to transform the project that ensued from the pedestrian to the inspired.

The first plan for Hart House was indeed pedestrian, providing no more than a single roof over a motley of organizations that needed accommodation. The building would be H-shaped. The cross-bar, containing an auditorium, ran north-south. The eastern arms consisted of the old red-brick gym and a new athletic wing; the western wings contained quarters for the YMCA in one and, in the other, a banquet hall and other rooms for student activities. The plan retained the old conflicts. A student approaching from the west had still to choose between wings, the spirituality of the YMCA on his left and secular pursuits on his right.

Ten months later, new plans were unveiled. The building had assumed its final shape, a rectangle surrounding a central quadrangle, but the spirit was still pluralistic. The YMCA held most of the south wing, the Students' Union most of the west. The existing gym was to be demolished and replaced with new quarters in the north wing. The east wing would house a dining hall. Within the south and west wings there was much duplication of lounges, common rooms, libraries, smoking rooms, and billiard rooms. Only the principal walls were as they would remain.

The physical character of Hart House was defined in one intensive year during which Vincent worked closely with the architects, Henry Sproatt and Ernest Rolph. Sproatt was one of the last North American masters of the Gothic form, Rolph a first-class engineer who understood design. Already at work on Burwash Hall when presented with this new commission, they produced a building of uncommon beauty.

By the autumn of 1911 the first sod had been turned and by August 1914 the walls were up and the roof in place. Then war broke out, and men and materials were required elsewhere. The House was pressed into its first educational service, training men for battle. Future officers were taught in its common rooms. The Great Hall was turned into a drill square, echoing with shouted commands and the clash of boots on marble. In the big gym, would-be aviators learned how to strip down and rebuild a bi-winged training plane. The future theatre housed a macabre puppet show at one end, a ruined Belgian village in miniature, its marionettes being German soldiers — targets for student riflemen posted at the other end behind a sandbag barricade. The officer in charge of this realistic rifle range was Lt.-Col. Vincent Massey; the designer and builder was a friend and artist, Lt. Lawren Harris. Later in the war, the House was used to re-educate wounded veterans in the use of their bodies: the swimming pool and common rooms were turned into centres for physical and occupational therapy.

The Great Hall is a reminder of those wartime years. One of the stone corbels on the east wall is of a marching officer cadet in uniform, carrying pack and rifle. Behind the dais, the Royal arms are flanked by the arms of the fifty-one universities of the British Commonwealth that were granting degrees when peace returned. The arms at the opposite end are of seventy-four universities of the countries allied to Britain and Canada during World War I. The gilded inscription that runs around the hall, taken from Milton's *Areopagitica*, is a reminder that even in times of danger it is important to study, invent, debate. More light-heartedly, corbels also portray Vincent Massey, his wife Alice, Sproatt, and Rolph.

During the extended period of construction, the House continued to evolve. The theatre, as the story goes, was added as an afterthought and quite by chance. One day Alice and Vincent were visiting the cavern that lay beneath the central quadrangle. Two great supports for the terrace rose at the eastern end. Both Masseys saw the outline of a proscenium arch, and so Toronto's first "little theatre" came into being. It was no small design feat, to build a vault across the width of the auditorium, add a green room, dressing rooms, and costume and property rooms, open two new entrances to the street, and install five hundred seats; but it was done. Such were the imagination and drive of the builders.

Three other changes were less substantial but more significant to the ongoing life of Hart House. The first was to turn over a lounge and an upper gallery off the Great Hall to the Faculty Club, which then had totally inadequate quarters in a wing of University College. (The Faculty Club remained in Hart House until the early 1960s, when it moved to its present quarters on Willcocks Street.)

The House soon after completion, seen from Queen's Park

The second was to transform a room designated for a library into a small chapel. This was a radical move. Although three of its colleges were church-related, the University of Toronto was by statute and tradition a secular institution. The architecture of the chapel was clearly Christian, which reflected the social ethos of the time, but it was non-denominational, and it did not contain a crucifix until a handsome example of contemporary sculpture by the well known British sculptor Eric Gill was donated by a visitor.

And, finally, as construction drew to a close, Hart House shrugged off its divided personality. The YMCA agreed to eliminate duplication of services and to restrict its operations to those religious in nature. The Y (succeeded by the Student Christian Movement) was given prior claim to certain public rooms when it needed them for meetings, but retained permanent control only over a suite of offices. The rest of the building, apart from the athletic wing, Faculty Club, and theatre, came under a single administration.

By the time it opened, Hart House was thus equipped to serve all aspects of the life of its members — their physical well-being in the athletic wing and their physical appetite in the dining hall; their social and educational interests in its common rooms and in other rooms devoted to music, art, reading, and debate; their spiritual life in its chapel. It had, moreover, extended its embrace to all constituencies of the university — undergraduates, graduate students, teachers, and alumni. It was, and remains, unique among the world's university centres in the breadth of its interests and in the scope of the imagination that created it.

On the first anniversary of the Armistice that ended World War I, 11 November 1919, Hart House was presented to the University of Toronto. As golden autumn sunlight streamed into the Great Hall, Vincent Massey traced the origins of the House and summed up its purpose, as important today as then. "The House as it now stands is intended to represent the sum of those activities of the student which lie outside the curriculum," he said, and continued:

A girl poses atop one of the carillon bells before they are installed in Soldiers' Tower.

...the truest education requires that the discipline of the class-room should be generously supplemented by the enjoyment, in the fullest measure, of a common life. A common life, of course, presupposes common ground. At this university it happens that but a very small proportion of the students can enjoy the advantages of the community life provided by a college. It is perhaps unlikely that we shall ever see in Toronto a completely developed collegiate system. But even if this were the outcome, there would still be the need, indeed the greater need, for the unifying force which it is one purpose of this institution to introduce into the university.

One significant constituency was excluded nonetheless: women. This did not stem from any misogyny on Vincent Massey's part, nor from unfamiliarity with women students. After all, he was, in his final year, president of the Modern Languages Club, where women outnumbered men ten to one. But he was a product of the Edwardian era, which ended in the same year as his graduation, and in those days women were accorded a special respect and separateness that would have inhibited the sense of community to which the House aspired. Regrettably,

Massey retained this view long after it had been relinquished by most of society. Only after his death were women, with the full agreement of the Massey Foundation, finally admitted as full members in 1972.

The House had 3,165 members in its first year. University registration was swollen by men returned from war, veterans of battle, eager to resume their education. They were tough and they played hard: some second-year students who had never seen the front lines tried to initiate the engineering freshmen, and were almost asphyxiated in a counter-attack involving gas. The first warden, a protégé of Vincent Massey, was unable to command the veterans' respect. He was gentle, amiable, witty, and knowledgeable, and a generation later he would be a well-loved figure on CBC radio; but in Hart House he lasted only two years. His name was Walter Bowles.

Bowles's lasting contribution to the House was to develop its committee structure. The constitution of Hart House, under which he worked, was based on three premises that had been determined by Vincent Massey and the university's president, Sir Robert Falconer.

The first was independence. The House would have the greatest autonomy possible within the university's larger structure, made practical by a system of self-financing through membership fees.

The second was that the House was no glorified student club presided over by an administrator, but an educational institution. The House's business was to educate students in what mattered outside the lecture hall, not merely to serve them. Its warden was to be academically qualified and was accorded a status equal to the dean of a faculty or principal of a college.

The third was that the House should be a democratic institution. Its life would be conducted by committees made up principally of elected undergraduates assisted by a few senior members—graduates and university staff members. The warden was to be deeply involved but as a guide, not a chief executive, and at most *primus inter pares*. The executive initiative lay with the committee secretaries, all students, who would also sit on the central governing body, the Board of Stewards. The warden's role, and that of other staff members, was to lead and persuade, and in the process educate. The system worked because successive wardens and committee members believed in that relationship and took their responsibilities seriously.

By the time Bowles resigned, the house, music, library, art, billiards, and graduate committees had been formed and the first elections to them held. (What is now the Arbor Room then housed billiard tables.) The Board of Stewards had been expanded to include greater undergraduate representation. The committees had assumed the initiative in organizing musical recitals, buying books for the library, sponsoring a masquerade ball, organizing exhibitions of art. The community of the House was emerging.

Then, in the summer of 1921, Vincent and Alice Massey had lunch with a young Englishman named Burgon Bickersteth who was visiting Toronto—his father and Alice's were old friends—and showed him around Hart House. The next day

Bickersteth had a phone call from the president of the university asking whether he would be interested in becoming warden. At first he declined, but fortunately he changed his mind. He was to become the second great formative influence in Hart House.

———————

Apart from stature — both were shorter than average — and a devotion to excellence, Vincent Massey and Burgon Bickersteth had little in common. Perhaps opposites attracted; perhaps Bickersteth represented everything that Vincent Massey aspired to.

Massey came, as we have seen, from Methodist manufacturing stock; he was an aesthete, controlled, a man who, even to his family, seemed always onstage, about whom an English aristocrat once complained, "Vincent makes us all feel so uncivilized." Bickersteth came from a long line of clerics prominent in the Church of England, including several bishops; he was a bundle of energy and enthusiasm packed in a wiry frame, a man whose actions and speech bubbled with an infectious enthusiasm.

He had grown up in the precincts of Canterbury Cathedral, where his father was a canon; he had attended a prominent public school and Oxford college. His mother had been one of the little girls who picnicked with Charles Dodgson (Lewis Carroll); she was said to be the model for the original drawings of the heroine in *Alice in Wonderland*. At Oxford, he had captained the rugby team and had displayed a stamina that in later years would exhaust many a Toronto man. In 1911, while Vincent Massey was taking a postgraduate year at Oxford once Hart House was under way, Bickersteth was braving mud and mosquitoes in summer, and 40-below-zero cold in winter, as a lay missionary in the lumber and railroad construction camps of the Athabaska-McLeod Territory northwest of Edmonton. During the war, while Massey was supervising rifle training in Hart House, Bickersteth was an officer in a cavalry regiment at Ypres, the Somme, and Passchendaele, twice winning the Military Cross for bravery. After the war he returned to Edmonton to teach at the University of Alberta. Two years later he was on his way back to England, having found no thrill in teaching, having almost died of appendicitis, and at the age of thirty-three thinking about a new career.

Once installed as warden he believed (or, equally important, appeared to believe) that Hart House was the most exciting institution, not just in the university or in Toronto, but in all of Canada; and he communicated that belief to everyone he met. "I was just thrilled every time I saw the House," he told me during a protracted series of interviews when he was in his seventies. Nothing was too good for the House, and nothing second-rate was acceptable. Very soon after he arrived he turned over the financial and other details of administration to a newly appointed assistant warden, Roy Gilley, later assisted by Rae Cowan; Bickersteth saw himself as an educator, and in the House he found the excitement he had missed in Edmonton. He had the wit to recognize opportunities and the drive to realize them.

He recognized immediately, for example, that Hart House was a natural picture gallery, a series of well-proportioned rooms with plain, light-coloured walls and

My first encounter with Warden Bickersteth was not particularly auspicious. At the end of a discussion in the Common Room in September 1929, I remarked on how dirty the wall above the radiator was. "I wish it were all like that," Bickersteth replied. "The place looks too new and raw." Hart House was then ten years old and he was thinking of the ancient halls of his beloved Oxford.

K.J. Joblin

generous windows. He had already met Barker Fairley, a professor of German at the University of Toronto, who was a vigorous advocate of the Group of Seven. The Group's work in those days was being attacked, far more than it was praised, by critics who compared it to "hot mush" and "a drunkard's stomach." With Bickersteth's encouragement and Fairley's guidance, and very much against the prevailing taste, the House slowly acquired the collection of works by the Group and their contemporaries that now is considered a national treasure. The purchases were made by the Sketch (later, Art) Committee, with expert advice — one or two canvases a year, using funds generated by the members for the purpose. In the process of selection, a group of interested but often uneducated young men learned a great deal about art; and, as the collection spread slowly across the common room walls, other young men came to appreciate the work of Canadian artists.

In his first year as warden, Bickersteth also met with J. Campbell McInnes, who had been a favourite concert baritone in England before World War I and now lived in Toronto. Together they planned an ambitious undertaking — a series of eight Sunday evening concerts each year in the Great Hall. The warden doubted whether the musicians of Toronto would be prepared to give so much of their time when there was no money to pay them. But they proved to be enthusiastic, provided that the audience was to be entirely of students, and the concerts became a fixture. Afternoon recitals in the Music Room, started by Bowles, continued. A Glee Club was formed and, in 1938, had its Christmas concert broadcast across Canada.

Bickersteth found in Toronto an American tradition of debating — teams presenting carefully prepared arguments before a panel of judges and a passive audience — and introduced the open, parliamentary-style debating he had known at Oxford. The experiment caught on quickly and captured national attention in 1927 when the prime minister of Canada, William Lyon Mackenzie King, spoke at a Hart House debate as honorary visitor. The Debates Room was packed for the occasion and the visitor was supported by a great majority. Other honorary visitors during those years included R.B. Bennett when prime minister, Agnes Macphail, then the only woman member of Parliament, and Ernest Lapointe, the leading Liberal MP from Québec. Occasionally the Debates Committee was attacked in the press for its choice of honorary visitors — the secretary of the Communist Party of Canada, for example — or of topics, as when the resolution proposed an end to imperial ties with Britain. The committee, and the House, weathered such storms.

These and other experiments are documented elsewhere in this volume. In them, Bickersteth was aided by some of the university's liveliest faculty members and a wide circle of acquaintances who visited the House, offered advice, and almost invariably were introduced to undergraduates. Because he believed so passionately in what Hart House was doing, he was able to persuade others of its importance and to attract an amazing number of visitors to the House. If possible, they had lunch at the high table in the Great Hall, where they would meet the members of all committees.

One such visitor was the great American black singer and actor Paul Robeson,

J. Burgon Bickersteth as photographed by Karsh

who after lunch talked and sang for half an hour in the Music Room. A friend of Gandhi's spoke to the men about life as a student in India and warned them that they would be unwelcome in his country because of Canada's immigration policies. Other visitors spoke of conditions in Arabia, Turkey, Africa, and China — all within eleven days. John Masefield, the poet laureate, lunched at the high table, as did Randolph Churchill, the philosophers Etienne Gilson and Jacques Maritain, Sir Robert Borden, the wartime prime minister of Canada, Arthur Meighen, then leader of the opposition in the House of Commons, Raymond Massey, in town to play Abraham Lincoln at the Royal Alexandra Theatre, Philip Gibbs, a noted British journalist who had just spent two months in the Soviet Union, and George McManus, the creator of a popular comic strip, "Bringing Up Father." This is only a small sampling of hundreds of such visitors, some invited, others coming at their own request. The Prince of Wales, the future Edward VIII, spent time in Hart House when he visited Toronto and played squash with some of the members.

To understand fully the impact of Bickersteth and his work, it is necessary to understand the character of Toronto and its university when he arrived. There were about 3,800 men students in 1921. Many came from the farms and small towns of Ontario and the Canadian west; a growing number came from the Ward, the area in downtown Toronto where many immigrants (in those days mostly Jews from central Europe) traditionally settled first. Many came from homes that owned a Bible and little else in the way of reading matter. If they knew any Canadian painting it was apt to be Paul Peel's saccharine *After the Bath*; more often they knew only muddy sepia prints of European work that hung in classrooms. In many cases, music to them meant no more than family or amateur or, at best, semi-professional entertainment. The radio and phonograph were only just beginning to carry first-class musical performances into every home. Radio news was in its infancy. There were no broadcast debates between political leaders, and public figures were not yet commonplace through television in the living rooms of the nation. Few Canadians knew much about the world outside their own continent.

Much of the informal education that occurred in Hart House took place in the warden's third-floor panelled sitting room, now named after Bickersteth. Groups of six or eight men would gather with him in the evening for coffee, sandwiches, cake, and talk in front of a fire. The conversation could be far-ranging. In one such evening reported by Bickersteth to his mother in 1933, it began with Dante's poetic style and went on to first editions, woodblocks, stained glass, psychiatry, the intelligence of ants and spiders, the missionary Albert Schweitzer, foreign missions, Christianity, peace, war, and aircraft. The men came from engineering, medicine, forestry, and arts and included the captain of the football squad. The talk went on till 1:30 A.M.

From all this — the committee deliberations, the parade of visitors, the talk at lunch and in the evenings, the exposure to music and art and debate and good books and the other many facets of the life of Hart House — there emerged a generation of Canadian leaders. The undergraduates of Bickersteth's years became federal and provincial cabinet ministers and politicians, senior diplomats, public figures in the arts, business, and industry, leading scholars and clerics. It is impossible to list them all, and unfair to mention only a few. They have often spoken about what

Hart House meant to them, however, and on the night of 11 November 1969 they demonstrated it. On that evening, a special dinner was held in the Great Hall to celebrate the House's fiftieth anniversary. Every living committee member, past and present, who could be identified was invited, and out of some 3,000 of them 600 came, from all over North America and from cities of Europe. Has any other division of the university shown such loyalty?

Vincent Massey retained his interest in Hart House throughout his life, during which he became, successively, the Canadian minister in Washington, and as such the country's first senior diplomatic representative independent of Britain; president of the National Liberal Federation; Canadian high commissioner in London during World War II; chancellor of the University of Toronto; chairman of the Royal Commission on National Development in the Arts, Letters and Sciences, which led to the creation of the Canada Council; and governor general. In his final years, completing the circle of life, he oversaw the building of another innovative structure in the University of Toronto, Massey College. He died in 1967.

Burgon Bickersteth remained warden until 1947, except for four years during World War II when, on leave from Hart House, he returned to England to serve, first in the British Home Guard, next as a civilian developing an educational program for Canadian soldiers, then as director of army education for all British forces at home and overseas. Before the war he had considered, and declined, the possibility of becoming provost of Trinity College (he was actually elected to the office and would have been the first layman to hold it), principal of University College, executive assistant to Mackenzie King and first head of the Prime Minister's Office (a position that was not created after his refusal for another thirteen years), Canadian correspondent of *The Times* of London, deputy director of the British Broadcasting Corporation, and a commissioner of the Canadian prison system. His reason was always the same: he was not prepared to give up the excitement and opportunities of Hart House.

By 1947 Bickersteth was fifty-nine years old and less in tune with the men who had returned from a second world war. He had always planned to retire at fifty-five and leave the job to a younger man. He had been warden for twenty-six years, just under one-third of the House's total life today. In retirement, he returned to Canterbury, once again dwelling within the cathedral precincts. He devoted his life to helping others quietly—to prison visits, working with some of the most difficult of prisoners, and to indexing the cathedral's medieval records for the use of younger scholars. Until his death in 1978, he particularly enjoyed playing host to visiting Canadians, especially those who came to him from Hart House.

Chapter 2
The Mutable Monument:
The Architecture of Hart House

Paul Gary Russell

Fellowship is life and lack of fellowship is death.
  William Morris, "A Dream of John Ball"

...that members of Hart House may discover within its walls the true education that is to be found in good fellowship...
  Founders' Prayer, Hart House

Hart House is a phenomenon. It didn't just pop up in Toronto scarcely a century after Governor John Graves Simcoe established his wooden stockade at Fort York. Rather, in form and concept, it had its roots in the Pre-Raphaelite and Arts and Crafts revivals of nineteenth-century England. It was, in Canada, the most fully developed demonstration in social as well as material fabric of a particular way of seeing things that was born in the late eighteenth-century revival of medieval culture and chivalric codes and blossomed in the last half of the nineteenth century, as articulated in verse, pamphlet, design, and image-making, by the intellect and sensibilities of William Morris (1834–1896). The poetic intensity of this romantic movement was early described in mid-nineteenth century literary criticism as focussing on the aesthetic of the "mutable moment."

The mutable moment, as it was referred to by David Latham in an essay in *Scarlet Hunters*, was the moment of opportunity or of keen sensibility, open to change in any direction. That moment, according to the critic Walter Pater, in his essay "Poems of William Morris," published in 1868, is inspired by "the desire of beauty quickened by the sense of death." This is the sensibility that imbues works of literature, art, and architecture, from John Ruskin, A.W.N. Pugin, and William

Morris in the old world of England, to Charles G.D. Roberts, J.E.H. MacDonald, and Henry Sproatt in the new world of Canada.

Hart House was arguably Sproatt's greatest creation and it is certainly the key monument, in design and social construct, of the Arts and Crafts aesthetic in Canada. The passionate sensibility that inspired its creation continued to be reinforced by the society of the House through its first eighty years, years marked by the awareness of death inculcated by two world wars and the necessary mutability of fabric and social form to ride out periods of change and adaptation while remaining integral with its Founders' Prayer.

This is an architecture that makes the mutable moment possible in the romance of its design. It strives never to repeat itself. Every niche and room is unique. The building, with its wandering passages and sudden vistas, stimulates with surprise and intimacy at every turn. This was, and still is, an architecture for comrades that encourages conversation, the chance meeting, the assembled argument, and the thoughtful meditation at different points in its varied architectural program. It is organic architecture in that its design grew and adapted during the course of its construction and is still open to change and addition today without destroying the grand pattern of the whole.

It is an architecture of welcome with many entrances, not an architecture of limited access and control, as in the classical vein of much of the modern design that followed it onto the campus of the University of Toronto as the twentieth century progressed.

It is an architecture in keeping with Canada as a northern country. If we appreciate Gothic design with an Arts and Crafts sensibility, it is not one of a range of styles to be selected as swatches from a pattern book, rather it is a social, aesthetic, and political statement in that it was seen as a group project inspired by the collective will of a community living in a northern land. Medieval architecture, with Gothic design seen as its highest development, was a northern vernacular, a natural architecture of space and light that adapted classical elements for northern countries of long, grey winters.

So much of the design, detailing, social form, and aesthetic of Hart House is inspired by William Morris and his Arts and Crafts fellow "art-workers" that these strands of continuity require a more detailed reference.

William Morris was an English designer, painter, poet architect, and philosopher, an aesthetic and political revolutionary. He was in his early years an active proponent of the Pre-Raphaelite sensibility to which he added, over the years, layers of philosophical, pragmatic, and political texture. He honed a personal vision of a life experience intensely shared by all. The way to that life was for all to have pleasure in what they do. That pleasure, when manifest, is art.

To Morris, all things done well are art. The stone carver, the gardener, the cook, the architect, are all artists, or "art-workers." All share in the intensity of art when they commit themselves to the pleasure of creation. Morris's Utopia was inhabited by a society of educated, skilled people making things by hand. The vernacular architecture of the north developed in the medieval period was seen as the germ of an ideal society lost during the industrial revolution. Morris encouraged his followers to go back to a future where art-workers grouped themselves into communities or guilds. These associations were by definition anti-industrial, anti-progressive (in that their ideal was a romantic view of the medieval past) and politically revolutionary, inspiring his socialist friends, such as George Bernard Shaw, to build this thinking into a political force.

Morris's epic utopian poem "News from Nowhere," published with a frontispiece of his own country house, Kelmscott Manor, is a vision interpreted for the New World at Hart House. Morris's social ideal, his idea of a guild of like-minded people inspired by the arts, working together for a better society, is rephrased in the Founders' Prayer of the House—that it may serve the university

> by drawing into a common fellowship the members of the several Colleges and Faculties, and by gathering into a true society the teacher and the student, the graduate and the undergraduate; further, that the members of Hart House may discover within its walls the true education that is to be found in good fellowship, in friendly disputation and debate, in the conversation of [the] wise and earnest … in music, in pictures and the play, in the casual book, in sports and games and the mastery of the body …

The mysticism of William Morris was inspired by the idea of north, as represented by climate, geography, and pre-Renaissance society, which he thought more indigenous. He found his inspiration particularly in the remote and windswept terrain of Iceland. In Canada, the artists of the yet-to-be-formed Group of Seven, including an articulate Morris disciple, J.E.H. MacDonald, went to Buffalo—to an exhibition of Scandinavian painting—and they were inspired to freshly interpret their north, their Canada. Excited by the contemporary Norse, they hauled their paint boxes onto train cars wending into the remote landscape of the Precambrian Shield. Appropriately, their paintings would hang in Toronto's new temple for all the arts, Hart House.

As Rosalind Pepall reports in her catalogue essay about William Morris, "Under the Spell of Morris: A Canadian Perspective," the products of Morris's design firm were admired and purchased in Montreal and Toronto as early as the 1880s. The Pre-Raphaelite and Morrisian love of all things medieval had already stamped the Annex, Toronto's newest and grandest suburb of the 1890s, with medieval vaults, carved grotesques, and stained glass—ideas transmitted to Toronto from England by way of Boston and its leading architect, Henry Hobson Richardson. St. James' Cathedral had been rebuilt with a certain bending of the knee to Pugin and Ruskin, in a glorious Gothic style, and the recently completed city hall and provincial legislature both acknowledged their medieval inspiration with grotesques and gargoyles abounding. The Arts and Crafts guild mentality also infused a growing circle of friends in Toronto's arts community. The Arts and Crafts Society of Canada was founded in 1903. In the same decade, Wychwood Park was developed by artist Marmaduke Mathews as an artists' community on a crest overlooking the city.

The last decades of the nineteenth century and the first decade of the twentieth also saw the arrival of Morris enthusiasts in Toronto. There was F.H. Brigden, who founded a printing company that treated its art-workers not as employees but

James Mavor

One of the stonemasons of Hart House at work

Sketches for stained-glass windows in the Faculty Club

as guild members; the just-mentioned designer J.E.H. MacDonald, who created book illustrations and decoration inspired by Morris's Kelmscott Press; and most important, there was the man in Toronto who knew William Morris—Professor James Mavor. Followed by his daughter, Dora Mavor Moore, and his grandson, Mavor Moore, he established a dynasty of cultural civic leadership and creative enterprise that would last a century.

James Mavor was born in 1854, in Scotland. After studying in Glasgow, he joined William Morris's Socialist League in the 1880s and began a long-term correspondence with the celebrated artist and poet. In 1889, Mavor became professor of political economics and statistics at St. Mungo's College in Glasgow. By 1892, he had secured a reputation as an authority on labour colonies, trade unions, and co-ops, who also wrote poetry and articles on the social and aesthetic values of the arts for the *Scottish Art Review*. In that year he was appointed to the chair of political economy and constitutional history at the University of Toronto.

In the next ten years he gained influence in Toronto's academic and cultural circles, with his far-flung correspondences with the likes of Morris, the poet Yeats, Oscar Wilde, Max Beerbohm, and Count Leo Tolstoy. He was known as a bohemian because of his scruffy dress and his forthright and radical (for Toronto) views on the arts and society.

In the first two decades of this century the tall, thin, amply bearded professor sat on or presided over almost every board or committee that ran an arts group in the city. Academic and civic groups sought his advice before any aesthetic decision was made. He advised on Hart House. In matters of design Vincent Massey consulted him on the crests that were to adorn the Great Hall. Henry Sproatt consulted him on the appropriate stone for his project.

Many debates on culture and society in Canada took place at Toronto's Arts and Letters Club. The Club was founded in 1908, the year of the first musings on a building project at the university that would eventually become Hart House. From the beginning the Club was very much in the Morrisian social mould. It was a loosely structured guild of art-workers. A May 1909 letter suggests that members should "come in studio clothes."

James Mavor was a member of the Arts and Letters Club. Over the course of the construction of Hart House and the war years, all the key players in the evolution of the House were gathered into the Club. Vincent Massey, the grand instigator, and Henry Sproatt and Ernest Rolph, the architects, were founding members in 1909; there followed Alexander Scott Carter, the decorator and illuminator; J.E.H. MacDonald, the graphic designer and painter, and all of the Group of Seven, whose paintings formed the nucleus of the great Canadian collection at Hart House.

Sproatt and Rolph had formed their partnership in 1899. By 1910, they were an established architectural firm. They created the fabric of Hart House, in consultation with the young Vincent Massey. Within the firm, quiet Rolph was the engineer, the highly sociable, pipe-smoking Sproatt the designer. When invited to build Hart House in 1910, Henry Sproatt (1866–1934) had established himself as an authority on Gothic architecture. Born in Toronto, the son of a city engineer, Sproatt articled in architecture with Arthur R. Denison in 1882. He went to New York in 1884, then to London and Europe with the architect Henry Pearson, before returning to Canada in 1886. He started practice in Toronto in the new partnership of Darling, Curry, Sproatt, and Pearson.

An early project with that firm was the design of the new Church of St. Mary Magdalene in Toronto. Henry Sproatt did the project drawing of a vast Romanesque monastic complex which was magnificent, but a far cry from the austere smaller structure that was finally built. Just two decades later Hart House would begin life as a relatively simple idea that gained momentum and financial support to become a much grander but still somewhat monastic monument to the medieval ideal.

As Sproatt developed his interests in architecture, his entire way of life became imbued with a deep appreciation of the arts, fellowship, and a romantic medievalism that we identify as the Arts and Crafts aesthetic. Critic Augustus Bridle described a visit to the architect's offices in the *Toronto Star*, February 11, 1922, when Sproatt was a local celebrity due to the success of Hart House:

He does his work in a spot that he and his partner purposely made a highly pleasant place in which to live, while you work. The offices and halls and library and draughting room are all places in which to live as much as possible as one would in a fine spacious home. In the hallway observe a fine fat picture of some medieval music lady done by somebody about the time of Frans Hals; in the head office, portraits of people along with the blueprints; in the library a huge handsome fireplace, stacks of readable books and places to sit and smoke; in the draughting room a perfect glory of light from glass walls; everywhere a certain joy of work under conditions that are favorable to the production of beautiful architecture.

Henry Sproatt's obituary in the *Mail* in October 1934 is probably a fair summary of how the architect wished to be remembered:

In private life Mr. Sproatt was widely-known for his kindly nature and gentle ways; a man who loved culture for its own sake rather than for any reputation it might bring. His love of learning and the aesthetic was manifested in the acquisition of books on architecture, art and kindred subjects; in the collecting of pictures and Chinese prints and furniture on which he was an authority.

The two press clippings together sketch a portrait of the architect as art-worker and aesthete. And this artist, like so many of his aesthetic medieval predecessors, had a patron—his own, then young, Toronto merchant prince in the Medici mould, Vincent Massey.

The Massey Estate's gift to the university was announced in 1910. The decision to hire Rolph and Sproatt as architects was made public at the same time. From the humble beginnings of a new YMCA and Students' Union office, the idea of

Hart House became very grand indeed; from an announced gift of $300,000 in 1910, to a building under construction, projected to cost $1 million, by 1912.

Even as construction began in 1911, plans were continually changing. Vincent Massey was always at Sproatt's elbow. As a newspaper of the time commented on the young Massey, "If he isn't up and doing when you catch him, he soon will be, for he takes life tremendously seriously and includes himself in a comprehensive survey of existence." At first the press reported that the gift was from Chester Massey and the Massey Estate. By 1912, the *Toronto Star* reported, "the building is being erected by Mr. Vincent Massey for the use of students."

Sproatt's eventual design is a free interpretation of gothic form in buff brick and Credit Valley stone. It was important to Massey and to Sproatt that Hart House appear to be what they intended it to be: a house, a large one to be sure, recalling the piled-up and added-to comfortable look of an English country house that had been built up by several generations over time. It would be a complex of rooms and passages simple in form but rich in the detail of significant areas and entranceways. It would be a very comfortable house, with fireplaces to stoke and sit by and all the amenities that a fellowship of members interested in the arts might wish to have. It would be their home on campus.

Of great importance to the country house is its natural setting. The precepts of William Morris celebrated the countryside, not the city. Hart House was conceived in a landscape, not on a tight urban street. Toronto in the early twentieth century (and much of it still is today) was very much a garden city. The university campus was then predominantly a landscape marked by outcroppings of structure. The site of Hart House had been, until a few years previous, open country. It straddled a creek bed and overlooked a pond that had only just been drained. The importance of nature as a setting for architecture was a given in Arts and Crafts sensibilities. Sproatt might well have wished to keep the pond, if it had been possible at the time. Architecture and indeed all art, thought Morris, should grow from nature. This sentiment, perhaps more than any other, was embraced by the arts enthusiasts of that time. Nature was Canada's leitmotif.

As the complex rose on its site, it developed slowly in an organic way, responding to perceived needs. At first there would be separate YMCA and SCM offices and a dining hall; then an athletic facility was added and it was decided that the whole would be a unified complex.

During World War I, as construction slowed down but continued nevertheless, Vincent Massey became a colonel in charge of musketry training in Canada. He was never far from the building site for very long.

The emphasis on craftsmanship in the structure was an early requisite. Stonemasons and woodcarvers, ironworkers and bricklayers added their talents over the decade of construction. When the House was formally opened Vincent Massey acknowledged their contribution:

If the direction of the building was sincere, the workmanship has been no less so. It too often happens in these days that the pleasure of self-expression has passed from manual work. On this structure, due both to the length of the period during which it was in process, and to the nature of the work

Vincent Massey, president (left), and the Executive Committee of the Art and Letters Club, 1921

itself, it was possible to preserve something of the spirit of individual achievement which is associated with another age. The craftsmen on the building, and I use this honourable term advisedly, have shown both corporately and individually, that the mediaeval joy of creation has not entirely passed.

In 1919 one of the first events in the newly opened building was a dinner in the Great Hall honouring the craftsmen who had worked on Hart House. In the decades that followed, this stress on the value of craft was a continuing focus of members' activities. In the first years two fully equipped arts and crafts studios were made available to members. As the century refined new arts technologies, they too were added. A photography club with full facilities was quickly introduced. Now a Hart House film board offers its own facilities to members pursuing the visual arts in the contemporary media of film and videotape.

When the Duke of Devonshire appeared before the crowds in front of Hart House on November 11, 1919, to officially open the building, Toronto's citizens experienced a degree of quality in concept, detail, and execution that they had not seen before in a local public building. They walked through a dramatically sculptured space with narrow, dark passageways leading to bright, light-filled rooms.

The main access was from the south, from Queen's Park. The House rose from a slight depression between small hillocks. As the visitor approached, the building's richest facade came into focus. String courses punctuated with a mediaeval bestiary act as bands that tie the elements together. Stone carvings over the main entrance at the west end of this façade, and on the bay windows of the principal public rooms, allude to the university's crest and that of the Prince of Wales, who visited just before the building opened. The emblems of military regiments stationed in the House during the Great War complete the heraldic agenda.

The main entrance portal is vaulted, and the visitor, once through the heavy oak doors, is confronted by a broad stairway leading up to the reception area and the Porters' Desk. A tall, two-storey arched bay window across the hall opens to the quadrangle. At this level the stairs split around two pillars which support the arch above and rise in reverse to a landing with a vaulted stone ceiling where today a solid wooden case is entrusted with the illuminated records of club and committee members since the foundation of the institution. Here the stairs reunite between the same pillars to form a broad sweep up to the second floor. The ceiling flattens out to a rich coffered pattern. The two pillars taper to the flat ceiling in a distinctly twentieth-century way, in this detail revealing the easy evolution from Gothic revival to stepped-back art deco skyscraper. On the second floor we are greeted by the upper half of the tall arched window, here capped by a rich oak frame.

The principal rooms of the south and west wings line the halls in either direction from this entrance and its landings. The rooms are all distinctive, but each has a fireplace and large bay windows, and most have finely crafted wood ceilings. The bronze chandeliers in the Great Hall and the sturdy metalwork light fixtures in the hallways and galleries are all marked by a simplicity of treatment

27

and a distanced reference to plant-like forms that allude to the Arts and Crafts sensibility.

The hall running to the east on the ground floor terminates in the lower gallery, a long, flat-roofed area open to the quadrangle. This is the dramatic tunnel-like entrance area that precedes the thrill of the soaring Great Hall, the pride of the House. The Great Hall, with its travertine floor, oak-panelled walls, and vaulted ceiling, focuses on a magnificent south window by the McCausland Glass firm of Toronto and is anchored to the north by a massive stone fireplace.

With the House scarcely furnished and open to the members of the university in 1919, plans were afoot to add more—a memorial tower honouring those 623 members of the university who had lost their lives in the Great War. This structure would be 143 feet high and act as a gatehouse as it straddled the road running north along the House's west façade. The Soldiers' Tower with its carillon was completed in 1924.

As the interior of Hart House was modified to accept a chapel, glass for its windows was collected from devastated areas of France, Flanders, and Italy. For the altar, a crucifix by English Arts and Crafts designer Eric Gill was presented to the House by Sir Michael Sadler in 1923. The furnishings were at first spartan, but custom-made. Straw-matted chairs—copies of Morris and Co.'s famed "Sussex" chairs—and high-backed benches conformed to the Arts and Crafts look of the place. But it was monastic: no window dressings, no rugs, no pictures on the walls.

In the next three decades, murals sprouted throughout the House. From 1934 to 1936, murals by Canadian artist William Ogilvie were added to the walls of the chapel. Art deco angels rise above the side wall panelling, honouring the altar.

In the archways of the Tuck Shop walls, pseudo-medieval renderings of academic figures held sway, and eventually a busy iconography of student activity spread across the north wall of the Arbor Room.

Commissioned in 1934, Scott Carter's celebrated map of the grounds of the university, in suitable medieval format, became the focus of the West Common Room and gave it its new name—the Map Room.

In 1929, the tenth anniversary of the opening of Hart House to its student members, the *Radio Times*, published in London, summarized the building and its worldwide importance as perceived at the time.

Architecturally of great beauty, and built round a quadrangle, Hart House is unique in that it houses under one roof a finely proportioned Hall, common rooms of every description, a library, debates room, music room, small chapel, together with rooms for the use of the Student Christian Association, two picture galleries for exhibition and practical work in art, photographic dark rooms, a billiard room, Senior common rooms, and dining rooms for faculty and also for Graduate members, an upper and lower gymnasium, both admirably equipped, separate rooms for boxing, wrestling and fencing; an indoor running track, a large swimming bath, squash racquet courts, a room for rowing practice, an indoor rifle range, extensive locker rooms, offices for the athletic and medical staff, a few bedrooms for guests, the administrative offices of the House, and the private rooms of the warden. Below the quadrangle is a fully equipped theatre with foyer, green-room, wardrobe and dressing rooms.

The *Radio Times* article then goes on to emphasize that the structure of the governance of the House is as important as its brick, stone, and mortar, then concludes with a warning:

> The care of Hart House and its welfare are in large measure entrusted to the undergraduates themselves, through the medium of nine committees on which, together with the warden and two or three senior members, sit students who have been duly elected thereto by their fellows... What might be called 'the Hart House idea' is being widely experimented with in the American universities. Something of a similar character is being planned for the Cité Universitaire in Paris, and it is probable that as the funds become available a building incorporating many features of Hart House may be erected for the University of London. Universities in the sister Dominions, in most countries of Europe, in South America and the Far East have requested and have received information about Hart House... It should, however, be remembered that the buildings for student life are a positive danger if they are allowed to become merely a hotel or club. The ideal which should inspire them cannot be more nobly expressed than in the Founder's Prayer of Hart House...

In the ensuing decades there were minor changes to the fabric and facilities in the House, but the committees structure held firm. During the Second World War, soldiers in uniform were again incorporated into House life, and later thousands returned after hostilities to take undergraduate degrees. In 1954, the Billiard Room became a coffee shop called the Arbor Room. The Reading Room soon lost its inglenook to office space demands, the old Sketch Room became a gym and a new art gallery, the Justina M. Barnicke, opened in the athletic services wing. The Senior Members' Lounge became the Gallery Grill. In 1995 a stained-glass window designed by Christopher Goodman and Angela Zissoff was installed in the Soldiers' Tower. Later, there were proposals for adding facilities on the third floor of the House, or expanding into the lane that runs the length of the building on its north side. Such developments are possible in harmony with the design of the original building, as its integrity is not threatened by such alterations or additions if they are made in sympathy with its established vernacular.

———————

"The desire of beauty quickened by the sense of death." Walter Pater detected this new and intense aesthetic in England over a century ago. In Toronto's academic community, Hart House endures as a monument to these contradictory impulses. When the building was opened to the public in 1919, it was criticized for its almost sybaritic richness. Yet its furnishings, although very well made, were spartan indeed. It is to this day a place of sensual enjoyment in music, the play, and painting, but also a place that evokes an almost monastic ambiance of contemplation in its inglenooks, beside its fireplaces, and, until recently, in the drifting haze of pipe smoke. It insists on the truth of Morris's conjecture that fellowship is life and lack of fellowship is death.

In *William Morris: A Life for Our Time*, Fiona MacCarthy sums up the great humanist's importance as "the way that he revealed to so many different people on different social levels such previously unimagined possibilities in life." The glowing torch of this Morrisian mission has been brilliantly passed on through the twentieth century by the architectural and governance structures of that most enduring mutable monument, Hart House.

Portfolio

Steven Evans

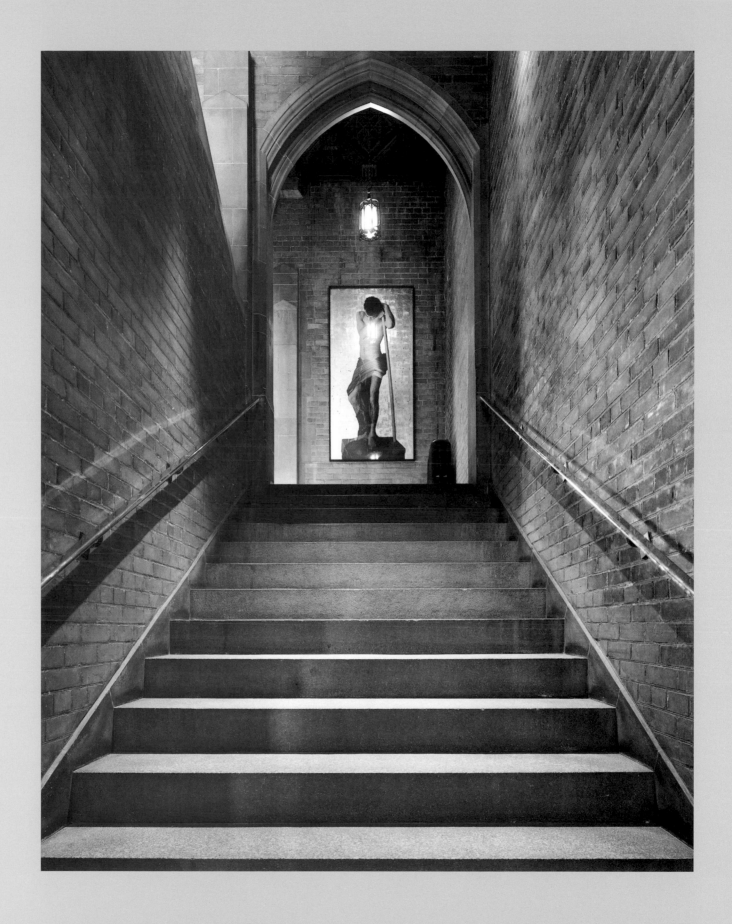

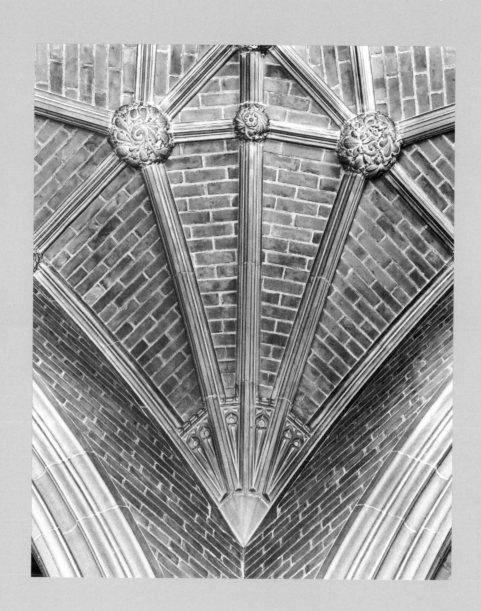

CAUTION DEPTH 2.10 M

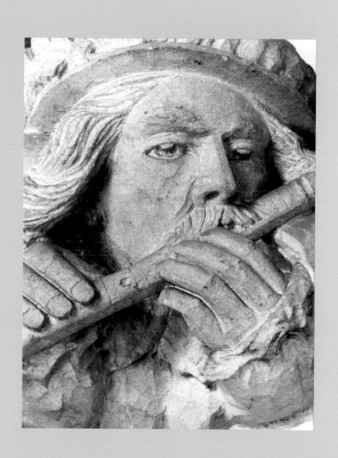

Chapter 3
Art: An Audience for the Future

Catherine D. Siddall

The story of art in Hart House is one of long and loving devotion by countless dedicated staff members, contributors, associates, and enthusiastic students. Starting with the founders and built into the fabric of the House is a deep respect for the visual arts and their significant, subtle effect on living structures, environments, and, most importantly, people. It is a story of constant support of living artists and of the presentation of their work and ideas to the university community. It is a story of debate and struggle with the constant challenges that artists present to established values. It is a story of traditions (as all stories about this institution must be) and a sense of constancy, stability, and comfort.

Over the past eighty years, Hart House has played a significant role in educating students about art. Not only were students offered classes where they could try making art, sketching and drawing under the direction of a practising artist, but they were constantly in the presence of "real art" while they participated in events and activities in the House. This more subtle form of learning—living with art—has influenced students' perceptions over the years and, often long after graduation, entered their conscious thoughts. Wardens past and present attest that alumni often remember and want to see favourite pictures when they return to the House after many years.

In accordance with the original mandate of Hart House, students form the majority on the Art Committee, which makes all decisions about art in the House including choosing exhibitions and purchases and organizing educational talks. (Although it has not been noted over the years, most students on the Committee were not and are not studying art or art history at the university.) This exciting, hands-on experience has often led students to take active roles in the art world as collectors, critics, and interested members of the public—it has even led some into careers as gallery or museum professionals.

The original, modest goal of buying contemporary Canadian art to grace the walls of the House has resulted in the assembly of a magnificent collection. As early as the 1930s, the collection was considered to be of national importance.

Hart House has played a crucial role in the Canadian art world and the smaller community of university art galleries—exhibiting, purchasing art and employing artists. One of only a handful of public art galleries and collections in Toronto, Hart House was and is an important venue for exposing new art to the university community. The construction of a climate-controlled, secure gallery space has greatly expanded the range of exhibitions which can be organized and shown.

In a letter to a reviewer in March 1930, Warden Burgon Bickersteth made it clear that Hart House was not open to the public (as was mistakenly suggested by the reviewer in her article) and this was "precisely the reason that so few articles about Hart House appear in the public press." In recent years this attitude has changed and, while the university community and House members still form the primary audience, members of the general public are welcome to visit the gallery. Exhibitions are regularly reviewed in the general press.

The history of art at Hart House goes back to the building's earliest days. The University of Toronto Sketch Club, which was established in 1917, was invited by Vincent Massey (who was listed as a charter member of the club) to use a room in the yet unfinished House. Because Hart House rules did not allow for the accommodation of exclusive clubs, the Sketch Club was converted into the Hart House Sketch Club in 1922. Later it became known as the Sketch Committee, reflecting its status as a standing committee in Hart House. In 1935 it was renamed the Art Committee. To save confusion I will consistently refer to it as the Art Committee, the name that is still used today.

During the first years in Hart House the Art Committee made a tentative start at its activities, including exhibitions in its Sketch Room, sketching classes, and the securing of funds for purchasing works of art. However, it remained for Warden Burgon Bickersteth to really breathe life into the Art Committee. He initially observed that:

> There is also a University Sketch Club which possesses a very beautiful room of its own [in Hart House]. The original idea was that there should be continual small exhibitions in this room which is specifically adapted for the purpose and also what is more important that it should be the centre of actual work—ie. a studio where at nights or at anytime undergraduates might gather and paint, draw or model under expert advice. This has not yet been developed at all. The Sketch Club is rather a dead concern.

But Bickersteth had plans which soon saw the appointment of Barker Fairley as chairman; the involvement of young, practising artists and professional advisors; the exhibition of fresh, new, Canadian paintings throughout the House; talks by artists and collectors to groups of students; offering of instruction with an artist in the Sketch Room; and the purchase of Canadian art for permanent display in the

Mounting an exhibition takes a lot of preparation, and even then not all goes according to plan. Ecological Ebb *by western artist Debra Cherniawsky was a case in point.*

As gallery director, when dealing with artists from other parts of Canada, I have to work with slides of the art and discuss the details over the telephone. The slides for Debra's exhibition depicted tanks of water with sculptural forms floating in the water. The gallery walls were to be covered with drawings that would appear to be reflections from the water. The exhibition dealt with the issues of pollution and the environment. It was ideal for a university campus.

Reality set in when the materials for the exhibition arrived: they included six large tanks, each of which was big enough to fit a six-foot-tall person into, with room to spare. These were indeed large tanks, much larger than they had appeared in the slides. So the challenge began. We had already figured out how to run a hose from the outside of Hart House into the gallery, so that was not a problem. What we had not figured on was the lack of water pressure in an old building. The water, at full blast, was nothing more than a trickle. It took eight hours to fill one tank, and we had six to fill in less than three days. The water was running day and night, as were we with buckets to other locations in the building to supplement the slowly rising water.

As people arrived for the opening, the last floating sculptural pieces were being put in place. The effect was worth the effort. The visitors to the gallery that evening were quite taken by the show and by the tanks of water. They did wonder how we managed to fill them up with water. I smiled and out of the corner of my eye caught sight of a bucket sitting under the reception desk.

Judi Schwartz

House. Bickersteth had known Barker Fairley as a student in Leeds and was determined to employ his interest and knowledge of contemporary Canadian art to invigorate the Art Committee's activities. In 1921 Barker Fairley was an associate professor of German at the University of Toronto. He had already proven his influence by helping to secure the commission of Vincent Massey's portrait for Group of Seven member Fred Varley in 1920.

Under the firm guidance of Bickersteth and Fairley, the Committee soon realized Hart House's potential as the primary centre for the visual arts on campus. It provided the only opportunity at the university for the practice and study of art. Furthermore, other than the Art Gallery of Toronto (later the Art Gallery of Ontario), Hart House was the only institution exhibiting and collecting contemporary art in Toronto.

By 1922 funds to begin purchasing works of art had been raised from the Hart House Masquerade Ball (the social event of the year at the university) and the Committee set out to the Art Gallery of Toronto to choose Hart House's first picture from the Ontario Society of Artists annual exhibition. A student account chronicled the event.

> Fairley of course had already made his choice and was way ahead of us, walking like blazes…J.B.B. [Warden Bickersteth] said, "Listen you lads. Fairley is the only one of us who knows a thing about paintings. We must be guided by him. He should really make the selection, but let's make him sweat for it." We agreed.
>
> When we arrived at the Gallery, Fairley led us directly to a lovely thing by A.Y. Jackson. We viewed it with derision and contempt. J.B.B. then led the group to something which looked like a spilled pot of jam, and we went into raptures over it. Fairley pleaded with us, swore and almost wept, then, one by one, we let ourselves be persuaded that his choice might have some merit. Then, one by one, we agreed that for once we would be guided by him. He marched back in triumph.

While the Art Committee had a democratic structure with students in the majority, this account demonstrates how decisions were often heavily influenced by respected senior advisors. Fairley, along with Bickersteth and Massey, ensured that the Committee and Hart House supported the Group of Seven artists at an early point when no other public institution, with the exception of the National Gallery of Canada, was purchasing their work. The collection was irrevocably focussed on the Group of Seven during the critical, early period of the Art Committee's development. (Eighteen of the twenty-six paintings purchased before 1930 were by the Group and its associates.) Indeed, the collection owes its current fame and national significance to this undisputed decision to support the Group of Seven.

Purchases were made carefully and money spent frugally (then as now) with Committee members and the warden often painfully aware that funds had been raised through students' direct contributions and special events. Price was a major consideration with the first purchase of *Georgian Bay, November*, by A.Y. Jackson.

The Art Committee's first purchase, *Georgian Bay, November*, by A.Y. Jackson

There were major works by other Group of Seven artists in this same exhibition but they were considerably more expensive. As it was, the modest canvas was purchased for less than the price listed in the catalogue. Bickersteth explained: "When they [the artists] realized that Hart House was forming an important collection of Canadian pictures, they were prepared to let us have their work at a much lower price than they would otherwise demand." While artists were not asked to lower their prices, they understood the value of the collection and the chance to create "an audience for the future," as Lawren Harris explained, writing to Winnipeg artist LeMoine Fitzgerald in 1932.

The warden, Fairley, and the Committee were intent upon filling the walls of the House with paintings and they employed ingenious methods to collect money for this purpose. (As Bickersteth notes, the House was offered many "artifacts" and mementos, many from the war that had just ended as Hart House opened. The House could have easily been filled with these gifts, but Bickersteth steadfastly refused to accept them, often getting into "terrific hot water." He explained that people seemed to "think of us as a museum" and therefore a suitable recipient of these donations.) In addition to the ball, funds were raised through other schemes initiated by Bickersteth in 1922. One method involved asking the presidents of the graduating classes to collect donations from students to be used to buy a picture for Hart House.

In 1927 an endowment for the purchase of art, established in memory of Harold and Murray Wrong, Professor George M. Wrong's two sons killed in the war, provided another major source of funds. This was the first benefaction of its kind Hart House had received. George Wrong was Vincent Massey's mentor and friend and his son Murray had also been very close to Vincent.

Although the Committee had been making regular purchases for the collection, it was only in 1925 that an acquisitions policy was proposed by a group composed of Professor Hardolph Wasteneys, the Committee chairman, Barker Fairley, past Committee chairman B. Richardson, Lawren Harris, and Vincent Massey. They recommended that it be "the policy of Hart House to form a collection of pictures representative of the best in Canadian Art and that therefore the purchases to be made each year shall be Canadian pictures." They also advised that a small sub-committee consisting of the warden, the chairman, and the secretary be empowered to purchase work on the Advisory Committee's advice. The Advisory Committee of three professional artists would be chosen by the chairman.

Wasteneys lost no time in inviting Lawren Harris, A.J. Casson, and Gustav Hahn to form the first Advisory Committee, announcing his decision at a meeting in January 1926. Harris and Casson, both members of the Group of Seven (although Casson's membership in the Group was announced only in its May 1926 exhibition catalogue) and the majority on the Committee, ensured that paintings by members of the Group and later their associates were well represented in the collection. Bickersteth, aware that the Art Committee might be open to criticism for favouring the Group of Seven, always endeavoured to have more conservative artists represented. In this case, Hahn maintained the balance.

Portrait of Isabel Nixon-Ralph by John Goodwin Lyman, c.1932

A sculpture show in the 1960s

52

The Art Committee, composed primarily of students, asked for the advisors' help when it occasionally sought out work of historic interest. Such was the case when the advisors' insider knowledge helped the Committee to find and purchase Tom Thomson's *The Pointers* in 1928. For years the warden and Barker Fairley had been actively searching for a suitable canvas by Tom Thomson to add to the collection. They rightly felt that it was essential to represent Thomson, who had painted with the future Group of Seven members up until his tragic death in 1917, in a collection that was focused on the Group of Seven.

The Committee learned that Thomson's sister was in possession of a large painting. She was approached by the warden and she finally agreed to sell *The Pointers* to Hart House for $1,500. (This approach had been suggested to the warden by Thomson's brother, also a painter, who subsequently exhibited at Hart House.) Although this sum seems paltry today for a work recognized as a national treasure, it was a daunting amount of money for the Committee in 1928. After long debate, it was agreed that Hart House must have the painting and that somehow the funds would be raised. The warden later recalled this purchase as perhaps the Committee's "greatest triumph."

The temptation to purchase paintings by well-established artists rather than taking chances on recently completed art by young artists has been an ongoing struggle for the Art Committee and its advisors.

A significant change to the acquisition process occurred in 1945. Students started to insist on having a greater decision-making role. No doubt, changes in the type and attitude of university students after the war was a factor. After discussions, which included the Board of Stewards, a sub-committee for purchases was struck. It included students who would receive "good training" and who would be advised by three artists. (A.J. Casson, who had served in this capacity before, was added to the existing artist advisors' group.) It seemed clear that this time the students would be very involved in decision-making.

After the arrival of Nicholas Ignatieff as the new warden in 1948, the purchasing policy was revised again to ensure a student majority on the sub-committee. The advisors were A.Y. Jackson, Douglas Duncan, well-known art dealer, and Charles Comfort, all of Toronto, with Robert Hubbard, curator of Canadian art at the National Gallery, and Arthur Lismer of Montreal. No longer exclusively made up of Toronto-based artists, these advisors would not wield the same influence over the students as in the past.

However, senior members of the Art Committee who worked closely with the students exerted a direct and powerful influence on them. Professor Northrop Frye, distinguished man of letters, became a faculty member of the Art Committee in 1943 and served as chairman from 1946 to 1950. His interest in Canadian art — the Group of Seven, Lawren Harris, and David Milne — was undoubtedly influential during his years on the Committee. The acquisition of an abstract painting by Harris in 1949 is attributable to him. This work was donated by the artist, who had held an exhibition of his abstract paintings in Hart House.

The practice of using advisors was seriously challenged in 1961 by students on the Art Committee. Today we would have to agree with the assertion of the Committee secretary, Barry Zaid, in his 1961 report that the Committee had not made very astute or important purchases during the previous decade. He wrote that "... the collection is almost entirely devoid of an example of the art characteristic of the '50s, a period most vital in Canadian art history." He proposed a number of reasons for this lapse, including a stinging indictment of the Advisory Committee. Zaid assessed the current method for choosing works as unwieldy and unworkable and the funds for purchases as sorely inadequate. (At this time, every member of the Art Committee brought artworks into a meeting towards the end of the school year, and from them the annual purchase was selected. One can only imagine the hot debates which usually resulted in the most bland, inoffensive art being chosen as an unsatisfactory compromise. Only $300 was allowed for purchases and Zaid recommended the amount be increased to $1,500.)

The activism on the part of the students led to a new process for purchases the following year. A small selection committee researched and recommended paintings for purchase to the full committee. During their deliberations they consulted with Alan Jarvis, former director of the National Gallery, William Withrow, director of the Art Gallery of Toronto and Professor G. Bagnani, a collector of contemporary Canadian art. This resulted in the purchase in 1962 of works by Harold Town and Jock MacDonald—the collection's first large, important, non-representational works. However, the change in the acquisition process was short-lived and the Committee reverted to the previous method of having Committee members promote their own choices for purchase. This method was finally dropped in 1977 for one that involved visiting galleries throughout the year.

After the Centennial year explosion in the numbers of public museums, galleries, and libraries, the Hart House gallery was no longer the lone, small public gallery venue in the city, but it continued to be vital. The 1970s saw the appointment of Richard Alway as warden and the arrival of Judi Schwartz as a program advisor to the House. Charity Grant, dean of women at University College, was appointed first woman chair of the Art Committee in 1973. Each of these members of the Art Committee played important roles in the significant changes and growth that the gallery and collection underwent in the following years.

Alway was a warden particularly dedicated to the visual arts. During his tenure he helped to build and open the new gallery and participated fully in all the Art Committee's activities. His special interest was and is manifested in his private collecting activity. Like Bickersteth, Alway has generously shared his collection with Hart House and has made significant donations in recent years. His collecting has focused on Canadian women artists painting in the 1930s, '40s, and '50s— an area under-represented in the Hart House collection—and his additions to the collection have helped rectify this imbalance.

The largest donation to the collection at Hart House was a generous bequest of paintings from former warden Bickersteth in 1978. He had collected most of these paintings over his years in Canada. They were very valuable, and several were major works by Group of Seven painters. His pictures brought great wealth to the House through the government of Ontario's Wintario program matching

At the opening of the Justina M. Barnicke Gallery in 1983, Donald McGibbon, Lieutenant-Governor Pauline McGibbon and curator Judi Schwartz look at *Open Window*, by Frederick Varley.

the dollar value of donations. The funds received from this program were to be spent on new acquisitions.

When the Art Committee learned of this tremendous windfall, a sub-committee was quickly struck and set to work searching out suitable pictures. Alway, Grant, Committee chair, Schwartz, program advisor, Anne Montagnes, senior member, the secretary, and another student made up this group. (I was fortunate enough to be chosen as the "other" student.)

The sub-committee, with the Art Committee's approval, defined areas of interest to guide its searching and buying. They agreed with the secretary in 1961 who had observed that the collection lacked works from the 1950s. For example, few representative works by Painters Eleven, an important group of abstract painters in Toronto in the '50s, had been acquired. This "gap" and others could be filled. The final list of works purchased meets the original criteria well, especially considering the limitations of availability and price at the time.

As the sub-committee got to work, many scouting trips ensued including visits to Montreal, Ottawa, London, Ontario, and many artists' studios. Sometimes providence seemed to be at work. In Montreal we visited commercial galleries on a tight schedule. In between appointments, Judi, Anne, and I ducked into a gallery not on our list and were faced down by a striking portrait by John Lyman. (By then we had seen a number of paintings by Lyman, one of the Québec artists who was not represented in the collection.) We gathered the other Committee members, who quickly agreed that we had to have this picture for Hart House.

In addition to finding historic pictures to add to the collection, true to the original mandate, the sub-committee purchased large, contemporary paintings as well. We saw *Homage to Van Dongen #1, Sheila*, a greater-than-life-sized watercolour painting of a reclining nude, while it was still unfinished in Greg Curnoe's studio. After much discussion, it was decided to purchase this large work even before it was completed.

The biggest challenge facing the Art Committee in the 1970s was delineated in an exhaustive report on the Hart House collection focusing on the condition of the works. Written by Canadian Conservation Institute conservator Elizabeth Phillimore in 1974, this report contained compelling evidence of the unacceptable risks the paintings were being subjected to as they hung throughout the House. After much debate, one of Phillimore's recommendations was implemented, and fifty-nine paintings, deemed national treasures, were sent on loan to the Art Gallery of Ontario.

It was always intended that they be returned to the House after completion of a space that would be designed and built to modern museum standards for security and environmental controls. No small feat. It would take six years and much effort and soul-searching on the part of Hart House members and staff, past and present, to accomplish.

Construction finally got under way in 1982. Much effort, especially on the part of the warden, to secure funding through private sources had met with success. The official opening of the Justina M. Barnicke Gallery, named in memory of

Joseph Barnicke's late wife, was February 17, 1983. The event was marked with much ceremony. The many invited guests, current and past members of Hart House, gathered in the Great Hall as Lieutenant-Governor John Black Aird was piped in. William Davis, premier of Ontario, presided over the ceremonies. Hart House members welcomed back the famous fifty-nine paintings to their new home with great relief and joy.

Under the direction of the Art Committee and staff, the gallery was ready to take up its central role in the life of the House. In addition to safely housing the permanent collection, this space was bound to re-charge flagging interest in exhibitions. (The Committee secretary had complained about a significant drop in the number of artists applying for exhibitions in 1980–81. While she attributed this partially to the growing number of alternative artist-run exhibition spaces, she felt there was also a need for professional staff to initiate and organize exhibitions.)

Now that Hart House had a specialized gallery space, it was clear that dedicated, professional staff would be needed to direct its operations. Judi Schwartz, who had been working with the Art Committee since 1975 as program advisor, was confirmed as the gallery curator/director soon after it opened. She was already very familiar with the House and gallery operations, the Art Committee structure, and working with students. The gallery director's role is to advise and work with students in a shared management structure while maintaining the high professional standards of public gallery operations required by professional associations and funding agencies. The job necessitates a sensitive balancing of often conflicting roles — professional and amateur, highly organized and flexible, didactic and entertaining.

Students continue to bring enthusiasm, energy, and commitment to their volunteer roles on the Art Committee, contributing many hours of dedicated work to the gallery operation every year. As in the past, their efforts are concentrated in sub-committees on exhibitions, acquisitions, education, and the annual art competition. Some students have specialized knowledge of the visual arts or art history, but many are from unrelated fields of study and are eager to learn about art through exposure and discussion. In fact, many of the past secretaries of the Committee (the most time-consuming, responsible student position — secretaries serve on all sub-committees and the Board of Stewards) have been from other fields such as anthropology, biochemistry, and adult education, to cite only recent examples.

The position of student keeper of the collection is a unique training opportunity with an honorarium attached. This job, with its very British title, entails working with the collection and House staff. Duties include curating exhibitions from the permanent collection twice a year, giving tours of the collection, completing collection records, participating on Art Committee sub-committees especially acquisitions, and working alongside the gallery director. Many of the student keepers have gone on to careers in the gallery field.

———————

Artists have always willingly lent their work to the House. The "Annual Loan" exhibitions, organized by the warden, artist advisors, and the Committee chair, were a vehicle for artists hoping to find a sympathetic audience for their work and

Within months of arriving at the University of Toronto in the fall of 1978, I realized I had made a terrible mistake. Although I had convinced myself that I would be suited for a diplomatic career — and had thus enrolled in the international relations program at Trinity — it was clear that I was fooling myself. The Hart House Film Board provided an invaluable community of fellow dreamers who had access to what seemed like the most sophisticated store of equipment that any aspiring director could hope for: a 16-millimetre Arriflex BL, a Moviola, and a Nagra sound recorder.

I shot my first film, Howard in Particular, *in and around Queen's Park and in various rooms within Hart House. As the film boldly proclaims in its opening presentation credit, it is A Hart House Film Board Production, and I remember being thrilled by its association with this most illustrious of cultural institutions. It was the equivalent of having my first film produced by Paramount or MGM. I edited it in a tiny room on the second floor of Hart House. Unfortunately, the room had a faulty radiator, so I did most of the cutting wearing mitts. That's why it's the only one of my films where you can actually see the splices.*

Showing the film at its glamorous, star-studded premiere was more exciting than the Oscars. It was the first time I had ever projected something in this amazing new format ... 16-millimetre! I thought it looked more impressive than a Hollywood Cinemascope epic, even if it was grainy black and white and you could see the cuts.

I can honestly state that if the Hart House Film Board hadn't existed, I would be doing something far more sensible with my life.

Atom Egoyan

also possible sales. The exhibitions, which lasted as long as five months, were a success, judging by the positive and detailed accounts in the press.

Small exhibitions were held in the gallery space. The emphasis from the beginning was to show new work, often produced by young artists. As a result, Hart House has played a formative role in many artists' careers. Even Group of Seven artists, such as Arthur Lismer and A.Y. Jackson, who were well recognized and exhibited, received their first solo exhibitions at Hart House. Because Hart House was extremely flexible, artists were able to exhibit work the moment they arrived back from painting trips. In some cases the paint was still wet. As an example of this type of almost spontaneous exhibition, we can cite J.E.H. MacDonald's exhibition of Rocky Mountain sketches, which were shown in September 1925, immediately after his return from his first trip to the West. This was his first solo exhibition since 1911, when he had shown his paintings at the Arts and Letters Club. The reception his work and his talk found on campus must have been very gratifying for this senior member of the Group of Seven.

Many contemporary artists, some of whom have gone on to great renown, have held important, often first, solo exhibitions at Hart House—to name just a few, Michael Snow, William Ronald, Kazuo Nakamura, Tom Hodgson, Dennis Burton, and Graham Coughtry.

———

The Group of Seven's strong influence on Hart House led to the exhibiting of many landscape paintings over the years. However, even when more "experimental" paintings were presented, they received an extraordinarily positive reception. Bertram Brooker exhibited his abstractions inspired by music in Hart House in 1931. The glowing review in the Varsity poked gentle fun at the paintings by relating a story about the perplexed Art Committee members unwittingly hanging several of the works upside down. However, what followed was a creditable discussion of the works drawing on Brooker's own explanations. The review concluded with the statement: "We are inclined to say that Brooker's work is a valuable contribution to Canadian Art because of its very freshness and originality." This open attitude to the first Canadian abstract paintings was not shared by the community at large. The majority of people regarded abstract art with skepticism.

Not all Hart House exhibitions have been received without controversy. Some of them have stirred up the community. In one such case, in 1955, Toronto mayor Nathan Phillips requested the removal of paintings of nudes he found offensive when he visited the art gallery. The paintings were taken down. A special meeting of the Art Committee was called and the minutes record a spirited discussion during which students argued passionately and well against such arbitrary censorship. They resolved "that after careful consideration the Art Committee of Hart House has decided that the present Exhibition will remain as originally selected."

———

In 1987 a major travelling exhibition of the Hart House collection of Group of Seven paintings marked the first time that these paintings had been shown together outside the House. Mounted by Oakville Galleries with Hart House's approval and assistance, "The Prevailing Influence: Hart House and the Group of Seven, 1919–1953" examined and documented the Group of Seven's long-standing relationship with the House. The exhibition, which emerged from a museum studies thesis undertaken by an Art Committee member who is also the author of this essay, was a monumental project for two small institutions, even with financial support from National Museums of Canada and other public and private sources. For the first time many people could visit the paintings they often knew only through reproduction as the exhibition made its way across the country.

———————

Although sketching classes were discontinued in the 1980s for lack of space and other limitations, the Film Board and Camera Club continue to thrive. And in recent years the instructional sessions and lecture series the Art Committee has organized have provided a forum for learning about current issues in art. As an example, in 1979 Michael Snow, an internationally recognized Toronto visual artist and filmmaker, was invited to give an illustrated talk as part of a series entitled "Modern Art: Contemporary Chaos?" which had been organized by the Art Committee student members. So many students turned out that the venue had to be moved to a larger room in the House. The series included a friendly, informative debate between Kenneth Carpenter, art critic, former secretary of the Art Committee then associate professor of visual arts at York University, and Sol Littman, a well-known art critic and journalist.

All members of the community are welcomed at Hart House, and in the 1990s the Art Committee has made special efforts to be inclusive in all its activities. For example, exhibitions of artwork resulting from cultural exchanges between artists from Canada and other countries have been held in the gallery. In 1998 the Committee organized a series of talks entitled "Out of the Closet," celebrating the achievements of gay and lesbian artists. As tradition dictated, this series of talks did not take a serious educational tone but rather sought to inform in an entertaining way. In the first talk, well-known Canadian artist Attila Richard Lukacs spoke to a large and appreciative audience in conjunction with his exhibition in the gallery.

———————

In recent decades, women have more than made up for their long absence from the House. Although gender is never a factor, the work of women artists is regularly exhibited and purchased, and women are well represented—often the majority—on the Art Committee. Of course, the central criterion for choosing exhibitions and purchases—quality—remains essentially the same. But in fact, even in the early years there were exhibitions of female artists, such as one A.Y. Jackson sponsored in 1924 of women painters of Montreal; and a number of paintings by women, many of them associated with the Group of Seven, have been included in the collection. (It should be noted that until the Arbor Room opened its doors the gallery was the only room in the House that women were regularly allowed to visit prior to being admitted as members.)

In the art gallery within Hart House, the management structure is unique in the Canadian gallery world. In many ways the gallery operates as a practical, living educational opportunity for interested students. The Committee is actively involved in every aspect of decision-making which is normally held exclusively by museum professionals and jealously guarded. As always, the success of this structure depends on the unique qualities of the House staff who are committed to shared decision-making in a co-operative, collaborative, working model. Hart House is a constantly evolving experiment in informal education, ever-responsive to the changing needs and interests of the students and the university community.

Margaret Hancock, the current warden, recently wrote:

> Many of us have not had the experience of growing up with original paintings on our walls, so it is momentous when we arrive at Hart House to discover that art is everywhere. A student said recently, "When I go to a gallery I look at the art, but when I am in Hart House I am with the art."

I did not grow up with original art in my home, and I now realize what a profound impact my experiences in Hart House had on me. To be reminded of this I have only to look up at the drawing on my wall by an artist I first met on a studio visit with the Hart House exhibition sub-committee. Meeting artists in their work environments has enabled students to gain a special insight into the making of art. For me and countless others, the many opportunities made possible by the Art Committee started an exciting lifelong dialogue with art.

Life drawing class, *c.*1970

Artist Attila Richard Lukacs in discussion, 1998

Testing Steinway grand pianos in the Great Hall

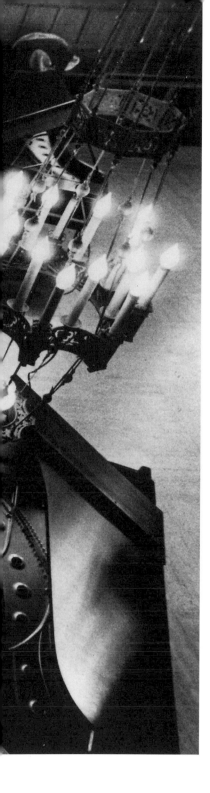

Chapter 4
Music: No Ragtime in the House
Jim Bartley, Brian Pronger, and Rupert Schieder

For some eighty years, a stroll past the ivy and hewn stone of Hart House has offered the promise of music drifting from open casements. The roster of professional, student, and amateur musical activity in the House has provided an ongoing, euphonious backdrop to other pursuits, as timbres of song, string, horn or reed echo down stone stairwells and pass muted through oaken doors. Many an anxious undergraduate has discovered a place of escape and renewal in the music programs of the House, whether as dedicated performer or casual listener. On Sunday afternoons and evenings, music at Hart House has traditionally enjoyed its most accomplished formal expression in the Sunday Concert series, presented invariably in the Great Hall, where acoustical warmth is complemented by the enclosure of timbered ceiling, oak wainscot, stone arch, and leaded window.

For many in the university community, Hart House's Great Hall is inseparable from the musical events that have graced it continuously for generations. Traditionally a handsome dining hall during the week, this room is perhaps at its best when filled with music—an apt accompaniment to the harmony and grandeur of the space. Few concert halls can match the experience of a burnished autumn or clear winter sun slanting through the Great Hall's splendid south window. At evening concerts, wrought-iron chandeliers bathe the hall in warm light and lift the listener's gaze beyond their glow to the vaulted ceiling, as if tracing the ascent of the music itself.

Music first officially graced the House in 1919, when bagpipers regaled the guests at a formal dinner in the Great Hall marking the presentation of Hart House to the university by the Massey Foundation. Perhaps in deference to the requirements of digestion, the pipe band of the 49th Highlanders played not in the Hall, but from the adjacent foyer. Three years later, on November 12, 1922, Warden J. Burgon Bickersteth presided over the first Sunday Concert, featuring noted British baritone J. Campbell McInnes, a choir of thirty, a six-piece orchestra, and two pianists. The music of Bach, Brahms, and Mendelssohn launched a series that became somewhat more eclectic as the years passed, and that has continued unbroken to the present.

McInnes was largely responsible for the push that got the Sunday Concerts off the ground. Then resident in Canada, he engaged Bickersteth in discussion on the future of musical life at the House. Funds were scant, and the warden was doubtful the place could attract enough accomplished musicians to sustain an ongoing series. McInnes would not be dissuaded; the talks ended in him guaranteeing his sponsorship for a year's worth of Great Hall concerts to be modelled on the Sunday Concerts held for decades at Balliol College, Oxford.

In his book about Hart House, *An Uncommon Fellowship*, Ian Montagnes quotes Bickersteth on the initial effort to attract performers, and the ensuing swift ascension of the Sunday series into the musical pantheon of Toronto's concert season. The passage reveals both the modest extent of Toronto's musical elite at the time, and a certain timeless immodesty that remains part and parcel of the profession:

> In the next few weeks I visited most of Toronto's leading musicians and explained what we had in mind.... Would they help now to get things started? They understood at once and asked only that we guarantee it be a student audience. Only one person would not promise his services, but within three or four years, when the concerts were established and it was an honour to be invited to appear at them, he then let it be known that he would be pleased to come. The committee replied politely that they would be pleased to invite him in due course.

Despite certain prima donna-ish absences, the Sunday Concerts were a great hit from the word go. Bickersteth goes on to describe audience demand as "enormous. We used to have great queues for tickets." Tickets were distributed free, limited only by the hall's capacity of about six hundred. (Of course, there was another limitation, not of number but of gender. Women, not being members of the House, could enjoy the concerts only on the arms of male escorts.)

The Sunday series has provided a continuous selection of music from varying repertoires for students, faculty, and friends of the House, presenting not only performers with established reputations, but also new and promising artists, many of whom have gone on to highly distinguished careers. Thus the mandate of the concerts has always been two-fold: bringing high-calibre musical performance to the university community, and giving early and prestigious exposure to rising Canadian talents.

The Hart House Songsters were formed when Hart House was still a male preserve. They gathered on alternate Sunday nights in the Music Room, when sixty to a hundred men would sit in the dark and sing. At the centre were a Steinway grand piano and an upright, with slide projectors beaming lyrics onto two large screens. Some people called the Songsters' evenings "glorified sing-songs," but what made them special was the leadership of J. Campbell McInnes, a leading baritone soloist and an expert on British folk songs.

There was perhaps a preponderance of songs from the British Isles—a natural result of McInnes's background. But I recall songs by Beethoven, and the American "Carry Me Back to Old Virginny."

The programs were carefully planned by McInnes in co-operation with the two accompanists. As one of those accompanists over four years, I shall always cherish the memory. Often the songs had been transposed down from available accompaniments so that the men would not have difficulty with high notes. Sometimes the only printed music was a melody that we had to harmonize. Sometimes the melody appeared only on the slides, and we would have to crane our necks to read it from the screen. Before this experience, I played only solo and couldn't collaborate with anybody. After it, I believe I was a useful accompanist.

Don Ewing

The historical influence of Hart House in the world of professional music has extended both nationally and internationally. Perhaps the most illustrious group to originate within the House itself was the Hart House String Quartet. In April 1924 it made its first appearance in the House, filling the five-hundred-seat basement theatre. The event was well covered by three Toronto dailies, and critics were uniformly laudatory. The review in the *Mail and Empire* was representative, noting that the ensemble "is unquestionably with regard to quality of tone, exactness of intonation, and unanimity of attack and phrasing the most promising organization of its kind that Toronto has yet produced."

Founded in 1923, the quartet was entirely the brainchild of Vincent and Alice Massey. The Massey Foundation continued its sponsorship for over twenty years, until the quartet disbanded in the mid-1940s. The original players, all faculty members of the House, were Geza de Kresz, Boris Hambourg, Harry Adaskin, and Milton Blackstone. They quickly gained a reputation as one of the finest ensembles in Canada, playing to capacity crowds at Toronto's Massey Hall, recording on the RCA Victor Red Seal label, and performing across Canada and the United States.

The Hart House Quartet was managed by the Board of Syndics of Hart House Theatre, an entity separate from the House, and chaired by Vincent Massey himself. Bickersteth is quoted by Montagnes as saying that the Hart House Board of Stewards "readily agreed" to the quartet's use of the Hart House name, but it's clear that the initial goodwill soured somewhat as success drew the ensemble further and further from its university namesake. Eventually the group was playing considerably more outside the House than in it, generally committing itself to only one concert per year in the Great Hall.

The Hart House Quartet's ten-month European tour of 1937–38 included James Levey as the new first violinist, Geza de Kresz having returned to his native Hungary. Concerts were given in London, Paris, Vienna, Milan, and Amsterdam, and even mid-ocean, aboard the French ship *Transatlantique* on the outward journey.

Whatever the tensions induced by a mostly absent resident quartet, they seem to have been resolved upon the musicians' triumphant return. The Music Committee minutes record a celebratory tea in the Great Hall in February 1938, attended by a broad mix of performers representing five years of Sunday Concerts and Friday Recitals.

Famed Canadian composer and choirmaster Healey Willan was another historic influence in the early days of the House, and his association continued on unbroken for nearly forty years. Willan first performed in Hart House in 1925, then only four years into his near half-century tenure at Toronto's Church of St. Mary Magdalene. His long-lived choir, the Tudor Singers, went on to become a fixture of the annual pre-Christmas Sunday Concert. When it disbanded, Willan brought along his accomplished church choir each December, and the tradition continued until 1961, when Willan was well into his eighties.

In 1954 a small string orchestra was organized by Boyd Neel, dean of Toronto's Royal Conservatory of Music. Bickersteth recalled that Hart House, recognizing the expertise of the group, "lent its name with alacrity, provided rehearsal space, and sponsored a debut at a Sunday Evening Concert." The Hart House Orchestra was soon giving five concerts a year in the Great Hall, and so quickly gained a national reputation that in 1958 it was chosen to represent Canada at the Brussels World's Fair.

The Sunday Concerts were by no means the beginning of regular musical events at Hart House. In 1919, as workmen still hammered and chiselled at the final interior details of the House, students inaugurated the Music Club. Every Wednesday at 5:00 P.M. in the Music Room, discussion of club business would be followed by a recital, invariably including a piano performance on the brand-new Steinway grand purchased for the House by the Massey Foundation.

Ian Montagnes notes that the minutes of the club's second meeting include the stern resolution that "all music of the kind known as 'ragtime' be excluded from the piano."

The Music Club, at first unacknowledged by the House stewards, was officially recognized in 1920 under Hart House's first warden, Walter Bowles. The club's executive was then approved as the Music Committee. Under Warden Bickersteth, the afternoon recitals in the Music Room moved from Wednesday to Friday, giving them, in his ords, "a weekend spirit" that enlivened the events and helped draw a larger audience.

The Music Room, long and narrow and well lit by natural light, is one of the most elegant rooms in the House. The carved and vaulted cedar ceiling seems designed to echo that of the Great Hall, and has the advantage of being near enough to the observer for the craftsmanship and the warmth of the wood to be fully appreciated. A central bay admits western light onto the resident Steinway from a bank of the House's ubiquitous lead-mullioned windows.

A wandering gaze during a Music Room recital is well rewarded by the room's unique touches. The timber ceiling arches are supported by carved stone heads of musicians, each with his stone horn, flute, harp or viol, and each worth a closer look when the music has ended. They are mostly rather smug-looking gentlemen in smart Elizabethan headgear, but for one cowled and mournful peasant by the south door, and, in a corner by the north fireplace, a wizened old man with a small pipe.

The Music Room has hosted an eclectic mix of amateur and professional activities over the decades. There was initially some emphasis on the informative, although Bickersteth reported that the word "educational" was avoided. Still, oddly enough, one of the more successful events in the early years was a lecture and recital by Sir Ernest MacMillan on musical structure which at times had his audience, in the warden's words, "roaring with laughter—for instance when he showed what Chopin might have done with the Funeral March."

A benchmark of sorts was achieved in 1932, when the Conservatory Quartet used the House's recently obtained antique viols to present a Music Room recital of Renaissance and Baroque music. The Hart House viols remain one of the great treasures of the House.

A climate-controlled display case outside the Gallery Grill has become the

I'll always remember my first visit to Hart House sometime in September 1956. While touring the building alone, I heard some unfamiliar music coming from a room on the second floor. I entered, as there was no sign on the door at that time, and discovered a new world, a treasure chest of long-playing albums along with the most comfortable leather sofas I had ever sat in.

I'm a Montreal native, and the Record Room became my home away from home for the next three years. It allowed me the opportunity to stop and unwind by listening to great music for an hour or two most days before returning to my rooming house north of Bloor.

Incidentally, the music I heard on that first day was one of Bach's Brandenberg Concerti, which to this day remains one of my favourite works.

Manuel Dalfen

long-awaited permanent home of these six ornate stringed instruments. After much debate on the relative merits and dangers of continuing sporadically to play the fragile viols in their original condition, it was decided that conservation was the wisest choice. The custom-made case in the Gallery Lounge is designed to preserve these Baroque instruments in their historic, unrestored state, while allowing for the possibility of future restoration and performance.

The viols were purchased by Hart House in 1935, though they had been stored and occasionally played in the House since 1932. The dark wooden chest that contained them slightly antedates the instruments, and has a carved inscription, "Margret Platts 1673". The chest was no doubt intended as a hope chest, and at some point was expertly refitted to cradle the six viols in a gently protective environment. The viols themselves, though not an original matched set, are a superb collection of individual instruments made between 1680 and 1761, representing contemporary musical craftsmanship from four European schools: English, Flemish, French, and German. Four of the viols are treble, one is alto tuned as tenor, and one is bass.

Over the years the viols have been used intermittently by music students and faculty of the university, and occasionally by visiting musicians. Their most notable professional use was over the course of several years in the 1970s by the specially formed Hart House Consort, at the time the only professional viol consort in Canada. It was led by Dr. Peggy Sampson, well known across Europe and North America for her performances on the viola da gamba. Under her direction, the consort gave recitals of Renaissance, Baroque, and even twentieth-century music.

The other in-house instruments are the pianos: a Steinway concert grand in the Great Hall, smaller Steinways in the Music Room and East Common Room, and several uprights of less illustrious providence. The Steinway history is of some interest.

The original Steinway, purchased in 1919, was almost from the start restricted to use by "qualified members." This officially meant that only students who had a specified level of conservatory training—generally Grade 10—were allowed access to the piano. Still, those familiar with the life of the House from almost any period know that one of its most enduring aural markers is the distant, echoing clamour from a pianist whose enthusiasm outstrips his or her accomplishment. The warden's apartment is above the Music Room, and every warden has at one time or another heard the Music Room Steinway in less than fine form. Bickersteth describes the problem, and his response, with characteristic diplomacy:

> Sometimes ... someone without permission obtained the use of it ... It was a very resonant building. Normally it was very beautiful to hear the notes of the piano coming up the stairs ... but if anything sounded odd ... I sallied down to see what was happening and they suddenly found me appearing round the corner.

Hart House Concert, Great Hall, 1964

66

The policy of keeping the piano locked was poorly enforced, and Music Committee minutes from many decades confirm this ongoing dilemma, occasionally acknowledging it as a sign of the House's admirable and forgiving inclusiveness. In the mid-1920s, the Finance Committee approved the purchase of Hart House's first upright piano, specifically (if unofficially) to lure jazz aficionados away from the Steinway. Even apart from unauthorized use, the Steinway endured a gruelling practice schedule. Tuning and other maintenance issues generated constant debate in Committee meetings. Minutes from 1946 note that in one month, forty-eight students had used the Steinway, most more than once.

The original grand was augmented by a second Steinway in 1949. Proper maintenance continued to be an ongoing problem, and in 1974 a sub-committee was at last formed to grapple with the perceived neglect of both instruments. In 1976 it presented a survey "of the pitiable amounts spent on these pianos over the years." It was the beginning of what became known in the House as "The Steinway Saga," an epic story of scathing Committee reports, questionable repairs, the embarrassment of cancelled performances, and even a proposed re-engineering of the Music Room's draughty piano alcove.

The Steinways were not concert instruments, being neither large enough nor in good enough repair for use at Great Hall concerts. One of the Steinway Committee's first acts had been to recommend the purchase of a proper (nine-foot) concert grand for permanent use in the Great Hall, thus saving the ongoing cost and inconvenience of renting pianos for the Sunday Concerts. The idea was raised on and off for almost ten years without success, until in 1984 approval was given for a piano "competition" in the Great Hall. For two days, seven grand pianos representing four manufacturers competed for the honour of becoming the official Hart House Concert Grand. Eight professional pianists were the judges, and the winner was a well-seasoned 1935 New York Steinway, then resident at Toronto's Eaton Auditorium. The owners graciously entrusted the instrument to the House on permanent loan, and it remains in use for all piano concerts in the Hall.

Sunday. It seems to me that's when some piano player came to Hart House to play jazz. Then, my love of music was latent, my experience limited to whatever records my parents had. But somehow I knew that the heavy-set black musician sitting at the piano was making magic. Today much of Oscar Peterson's music is captured in the many compact discs slotted beside a sound system that honours them.

Dave Hunter

Live performance and listening have always, by a large margin, been the principal focus of music programs at Hart House. Still, as recording technology grew increasingly sophisticated in the 1930s and '40s, there were suggestions from members of installing phonograph equipment and buying records to stock a listening library. Warden Bickersteth describes the response: "The Music Committee set its face against 'mechanical music' in Hart House for a long time." The feeling was that musicians who gave their time and talent, for usually quite a minimal honorarium, would be less likely to do so if their own (or perhaps better) performances were readily available in the record library. This was eventually recognized as a false fear, and in the mid-1940s there began serious plans for a record room. The project was officially approved in 1947.

The House's card room was chosen for several reasons: it was the ideal size, it could be easily adapted for soundproofing, and the new use would put an end to what was perceived as a growing gambling problem among some members — in particular certain ex-servicemen who seemed to lose, in Bickersteth's words, "an entire month's government allowance as soon as the cheques arrived."

A Music Committee member who had recently graduated in electrical engineering was commissioned to design and build the phonograph system. After an inaugural test of the equipment in the Great Hall, in which records were played for a small audience, the Record Room was opened in 1948. Less than a year later, it was reported to be in use an average of twelve hours a day. In the 1960s, acknowledging evolving musical tastes, a second Record Room was set up, and its shelves stocked with a growing collection of jazz and folk music, while the original room's stock of classical music continued to expand.

Over the years equipment was upgraded, and with the advent of compact disc technology the collection was reintegrated into one room. It now contains some three thousand vinyl records and an expanding inventory of nearly three hundred CDs, representing a broad range of classical, jazz, folk, pop, and rock, and a selection of traditional music from various cultures.

Members wanting to use the Record Room undergo a brief training session in the use of the equipment, and are issued a card which allows them access to the room key. There has always been a time limit on individual use. For several decades the room could be locked from the inside, assuring a privacy that encouraged some members of the House to fully utilize the intimacy of the space, while the strains of Mozart or Gershwin or Iggy Pop provided a sort of cover. (Other covers have been used in a pinch. Music Committee minutes mention one couple hiding their shame beneath a handy piano cover when a cleaning staffer entered unexpectedly. "Inappropriate use" was the Committee's measured assessment of the incident.)

———

The year 1957 brought an unprecedented change to the musical life of the House. After much discussion and many failed proposals, the Jazz Sub-Committee was formed in the spring, and by that summer had resolved that three jazz recitals should be mounted in the next academic year. The Peter Appleyard Quartet gave a distinguished launch to the series, drawing a large crowd to the Music Room. The lesser-known Alf Coward Trio followed, while in spring 1958 Moe Kaufman had appreciative House members overflowing into the corridors. Despite the initial reluctance of some Committee members to allow jazz in the hallowed Great Hall, within a few years Oscar Peterson had appeared in the Hall, filling it to capacity in 1961.

Jazz, not to mention ragtime, has flourished in the House ever since. By 1975 up to twenty concerts per academic year were on offer, and 1977 saw the first summer series planned specifically for the Hart House quadrangle, with jazz augmented by pop and classical. The high point was a week-long event, "A Jazz Festival," featuring workshops and concerts in the House with John Arpin, Phil Nimmons, Ted Moses, and Jim Galloway, and ending with a return appearance by Moe Koffman, this time in Convocation Hall. The ongoing Jazz Plus series, begun in the 1980s, was renamed Jazz at Oscar's in 1991, and remains a Friday night fixture in the Arbor Room.

The idea that jazz might not be too radical an innovation opened the door to other musical expression from the 1960s onward, giving pop and rock performers increasing exposure in the House, often in series or single events staged in the Arbor Room or outdoor in the quadrangle.

Music of varying cultures has also been programmed. In 1970 a program of classical Indian music drew a large crowd to the Music Room. Ensuing years have brought appearances in the Great Hall by groups as diverse as the Classical Arab Music Quintet and a Balinese gamelan ensemble, which encouraged audience members to participate in the extensive percussion section. A benchmark event was 1981's Music of the World's Peoples series, offering West African, North Indian, traditional Chinese, and Greek folk music.

The music of Hart House has literally been heard across Canada, thanks to an ongoing collaboration between the Music Committee and CBC Radio which has spanned more than forty years.

The first House event broadcast on radio was an isolated and impromptu affair. In 1938 the Hart House Glee Club presented Christmas carols in the Great Hall one lunch hour at the end of the fall term. There happened to be some CBC officials attending, and one of them is reported by Warden Bickersteth as saying, "We want to reproduce this entire scene and broadcast it tomorrow from Halifax to Victoria." The next afternoon a live broadcast introduced Hart House to a nation of radio listeners with some brief sounds of clattering dishes and mealtime chatter from the Great Hall, followed by four carols sung by the Glee Club and another by the entire assembled company.

Extensive radio collaboration began in 1958, when the CBC approached the Music Committee and proposed a series of concerts to be broadcast from Hart House. Maureen Forrester was one of the first artists to be heard nationally from the Great Hall. It was a unique liaison that spread the reputation of the House across Canada and further enabled university audiences to hear artists of consummate skill and reputation. Among other well-known performers, the series has over the years presented Joan Sutherland, Andres Segovia, Janos Starker, Benno Moiseiwitch, Rudolf Furkusny, Robert Aitken, Betty Jean Hagen, Leo Barkin, Lois Marshall, William Aide, Anton Kuerti, Greta Kraus, Galina Vishnevskaya, and Mstislav Rostropovich.

The CBC liaison has been highly successful in giving House members more exposure to artists of international stature, both from within and outside Canada. The greatest disadvantage has perhaps been the erosion of the Music Committee's artistic control, especially on the issue of who performs in the Great Hall. When the CBC is involved in a concert, Hart House essentially has to take whatever program is on offer. Though this has ruffled some feathers on occasion, the results have most often been worth the slight friction.

In 1992, CBC producers found themselves in possession of a new Toronto concert and broadcast facility, the Glenn Gould Studio. This significantly dampened their interest in liaising with Hart House, but the collaboration has lately enjoyed a gratifying revival, which shows every sign of continuing.

Lois Marshall after giving a recital for the House's fiftieth anniversary celebrations

Gould himself made one of his earliest public appearances at Hart House, in the Music Room, in February 1949. He was sixteen. A Great Hall concert followed a year later. He continued to be sought after for Hart House appearances throughout the 1950s, but his rapid ascent to fame rendered these approaches fruitless. Through great effort he was nearly booked for the 300th Sunday Concert in 1960, but dates could finally not be juggled to meet his heavy schedule. Leo Barkin appeared in his stead before an appreciative crowd. Gould did pay one other notable, if vicarious, visit to the House, in 1975. Before a packed Music Room, the noted philosophy scholar Geoffrey Payzant presented an engaging and highly praised lecture and exegesis on the life and work of Gould, using audio tapes, film clips, and recordings. The result a few years later was Payzant's definitive book on the brilliant and eccentric Gould — *Glenn Gould: Music and Mind*.

Many other noted artists and special series have enriched the Sunday Concerts. In 1973 the Czech Quartet presented a musical history of the development of the string quartet as a form, including lively commentary by Richard Gale. The 1974–75 season saw the performance by Anton Kuerti of the complete Beethoven piano sonatas and the Diabelli Variations, in a series of ten weekly concerts. Attendance was near capacity for the entire series, averaging between five hundred and six hundred per performance. Kuerti later recorded the complete sonatas along with his own commentary as prepared for the Great Hall audiences, resulting in a unique musical resource that continues to be used in schools and libraries. Other notable events include 1978's "Beethoven at Hart" series, presenting the complete sonatas for violin and piano, and for cello and piano, performed by Elyakim Taussig, Otto Armin, and Tsuyoshi Tsutsumi, as well as the 1980 "Mendelssohn at Hart" program featuring the university's distinguished long-time quartet-in-residence, the Orford String Quartet. Both of these series were broadcast later on CBC Stereo.

The 350th Sunday Concert in 1967 brought Maureen Forrester back to the House for a centennial-year tribute. In 1974 the 400th Concert featured, among others, Robert Aitken, Betty Jean Hagen, and Lois Marshall. The 500th Concert saw the return in 1989 of the Orford Quartet for a program of Haydn and Beethoven, and an R. Murray Schafer piece commissioned by the CBC specially for the Orford. The list of illustrious names from almost eight decades of Great Hall concerts forms a professional roll of honour from Canadian and world music. To select just a few not yet mentioned, from a long list: Sir Ernest MacMillan, the Toronto Consort, the Hart House Chorus, the Elmer Eisler Singers, the Canadian Brass, Tafelmusik, the St. Lawrence Quartet, Ofra Harnoy, Stuart Hamilton, Jan Rubes, Jon Vickers, and Mario Bernardi.

Still, the honoured and venerable have had far from a monopoly on the Sunday Concerts. Under Warden Jean Lengellé, the very important "debut" series was launched, renewing the emphasis on providing a venue for unknown, promising young artists. The mandate of the Music Committee continues to strongly reflect this commitment.

On another level, the Committee has always had a symbiotic relationship with the Faculty of Music. No other standing committee has had such a direct link to the professional world and another jurisdiction within the university. Many of the past chairs have been distinguished musicians and also teachers at the Faculty —

(Facing page) A CBC recording session with the Hart House Orchestra

from Sir Ernest MacMillan to the present faculty advisor Cameron Walter—and, of course, many of the graduating students give their final recitals in Hart House.

All committees at the House are made up of unpaid volunteers, and the Music Committee is no exception.

Officially, if not in practice, no musical event can occur in the House outside the purview or the direct instigation of the Committee. The level of commitment this demands has always been formidable, and sometimes gruelling. One of the great achievements of the ongoing Hart House experiment has been the dedication inspired in its army of volunteers. (This is not idle boosterism. Consider that all of the House events and programs described above came into being essentially through volunteer labour, from conception through planning, from negotiation with artists through the often precarious budgeting of each season.)

In 1994 one of the Committee's most tireless chairs—and by far its longest-serving—Rupert Schieder retired at the age of eighty. The final Sunday Concert of each season is now dedicated in his honour.

Hart House Chorus rehearsal, 1974

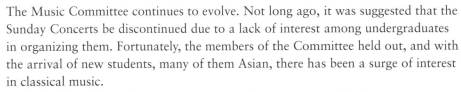

The Music Committee continues to evolve. Not long ago, it was suggested that the Sunday Concerts be discontinued due to a lack of interest among undergraduates in organizing them. Fortunately, the members of the Committee held out, and with the arrival of new students, many of them Asian, there has been a surge of interest in classical music.

Each of the Music Committee's sub-committees is responsible for a particular series or facility at the House. This year the diversity of backgrounds and experiences among the sub-committee chairs reflects the growing inclusiveness of the House. The Sunday Concert co-chairs are Chinese and Vietnamese; the Record Room chair is Filipino; Jazz at Oscar's is chaired by an African Canadian; the Noon Hour Concerts sub-committee is chaired by a Chinese student; and the Music Committee secretary is Lithuanian. The leadership and vitality within the House today come from such diversity.

Independent of the Music Committee, musical clubs of House members have flourished without pause since students formed the prototype music club in 1919. Six of the twenty-three clubs now active at Hart House are devoted exclusively to music. Altogether, their members number almost a thousand. There are four instrumental ensembles and two choral groups.

Originally an offspring of the Music Committee, the Hart House Orchestra has long been autonomous. Under the baton of Errol Gay, the present orchestra, unlike its precursor of the 1950s, is not a string ensemble but a seventy-five-piece symphony orchestra including winds, brass, and percussion. It gives three concerts per year in the Great Hall. Comprising students, faculty, staff, and alumni, it is intergenerational and multicultural—a true community orchestra.

The other instrumental ensembles all evolved from the orchestra. The Chamber Strings, conducted and coached by Fabio Mastrangelo, is a small group of amateurs performing works from the Baroque to contemporary. It gives concerts twice a year in the Great Hall. The Jazz Ensemble is devoted to big-band jazz music, with conductor Josh Grossman leading a group of musicians ranging from novice to veteran. A concert in the Arbor Room marks the end of each term. The Symphonic Band is led by Keith Reid, and comprises sixty musicians playing an array of twenty band instruments. It performs twice a year in the House.

The Hart House Chorus, which evolved from the old Glee Club, is a long-lived group with a history of successful touring in Canada and abroad. Directed for over ten years by renowned organist John Tuttle, the sixty-member chorus recruits by audition, performs two Great Hall concerts per year, and participates in the Inter-Varsity Choral Festival. It has performed on television and radio, and at this writing is planning another European tour.

The Singers is a group dedicated to those who love to sing, but balk at the prospect of an audition. Directed by Melva Treffinger Graham, its members are less daunted by collective performance, giving a concert in the Great Hall at the end of each term.

And then there are the regular series. Three regular weekly events draw large crowds from across the university. The Thursday Night Open Stages in the Arbor Room attract undergraduates who turn up with their guitars and fiddles and even drums. Jazz at Oscar's on Friday nights, underwritten by the Musicians' Trust, is an established venue for distinguished jazz musicians. The weekly Noon Hour Concerts are often broadcast by CFRB and CBC 2.

Last year the House hosted a new Tuesday night recital series in partnership with the Faculty of Music, and co-sponsored "Worlds of Music," a very popular workshop series which covered everything from African drumming to Inuit throat singing.

Tradition at Hart House has produced both harmony and discord. The full admission of women to the House, in 1972, certainly ought to have occurred fifty-three years earlier when Hart House opened. In 1995 Anne Gibson achieved a long-overdue breakthrough by becoming the first woman chair of the Music Committee. Music, the universal language, easing the shackles of that enforced inequity, has brought men and women together in Hart House for eight decades. Warden Bickersteth, whose spirit of inclusion warmed the life of the House for more than two decades, seemed delighted when he could report that the "lads" at a particular concert or lecture were equalled in number by their "girls." The language is now quaint, but the impulse remains the essence of Hart House, at last fully realized: a place of welcome, camaraderie, and community.

Drawing of Harcourt Brown in the Library, by J.E.H. MacDonald, 1925

Chapter 5
Literature:
Hanging Out with Hemingway

Bruce Meyer

Hart House is the most organic of all the University of Toronto's parts, a living institution much like a human body. The Library is the memory of this living entity, its conscience and its voice. For many, such as novelist Morley Callaghan, who attended the university during Hart House's first years, the Library is a special place. Writing in his 1948 novel, *The Varsity Story*, the Library is portrayed in a magical, ethereal way: "There in the quiet Library, with the sunlight glinting on the red sofa and the natural wood panelling, all was bathed in a soft glow, and it became a world in which he experienced a strange elation; he would feel capable of sharing in the bewildering creative vision of a great writer." As current program advisor Patricia Grant pointed out, "the Library is a living library where the printed word leaps off the page." Indeed, it has been a place where writers and those who simply love books have come to dream of the universe of language and the great undiscovered worlds that lie on the horizons of the imagination. Of all the rooms in the House, the Library is a place where the inner expression, the private person, the self, is balanced against the demands and rigours of university life.

My own introduction to the Library was not quite as magical or even as memorable as that moment articulated by Callaghan. "You'd better make sure you take the Hart House tour," my college's registrar advised me during a welcome gathering of cookies and lemonade. As a dutiful young recruit to the academic world in the mid-1970s, I obeyed. The next day, a slightly pudgy young man met a group of us at the porter's desk at the appointed time. He had an energetic glow about him, a zealous pride in the place he was charged to display to the novices. We snaked our way through the corridors on what seemed like a tour of an English great house rather than a university facility for students. The emptiness of the Debates Room and the Music Room was slightly off-putting. The Reading Room seemed interesting enough with its racks of magazines and newspapers until our guide added, "We discourage studying here. Hart House is a place for people to come relax and enjoy themselves." Relax? Enjoy? I was shocked. I thought I had come to university to succeed or die trying.

We made our way upstairs. The guide opened a narrow oak door and its leaded glass rattled. "This," he said with his eyes almost bulging from his head and with an extra note of reverence in his voice, "this is the Library." A hushed silence, as at the tomb of a great statesman, fell over the tour. "None of the books here are of a scholarly nature. These are intended for reading enjoyment rather than for study."

I was appalled. It seemed like such a waste of time to read just for enjoyment. I had a world to win. The Robarts was calling to me. My *Norton Anthology of Major British Authors* was fresh off the shelf at the bookstore. "Do people have time to read for pleasure here?" I asked incredulously. "The sane ones do," replied the shining scout.

Two portraits adorned the far end of the room—one of a distinguished-looking man in a dress uniform with his body almost draped over his chair in an uncharacteristically casual fashion, and the other of a woman, presumably his wife, slightly erect, as if about to interject an amusing though not profound comment on the proceedings of a sophisticated evening. There was an upper-year student flaked out on one of the burgundy leather couches, his arm sprawled almost to the floor in a gesture of melancholy, almost Pre-Raphaelite death. "We really don't encourage sleeping here," added the guide and he coughed as if to make his point to the sleeper. If snoozing wasn't in order, I wondered if the two memorialized souls at the head of the room set the tone for the place, and I filed away in my over-packed and overawed freshman mind the concept that the Library was for "stylish" events, a la Noel Coward. As the September morning sun filtered through the leaded glass windows and we left the sleeper in his deep, sepulchral silence, it donned on me that here was a place that I might be able to come to get away from things, if and when I found the need to shut the world out.

As we filed out, I turned to my host. "I don't suppose one could write poems here?" I was expecting a negative answer.

"On the contrary, we encourage that sort of thing here, as long as it isn't for a course." And that was my introduction to Hart House Library. I didn't make it back for some time. A year later, when my Shakespeare tutorial leader accused me of writing "poetry rather than analytical prose" on an essay, I made my way through a November blizzard to the Library and took refuge in a place where dreams were possible and poetry was permitted.

―――――――

Over the years, the Library has never lost that sense of beautiful peace that I discovered that first, hot September morning in the mid-1970s. In its most recent "Mission Statement," the Library Committee, the brains, guts, soul, and hard work behind that solitude, declared that it is "committed to supporting the literary endeavours of the university, and of the larger Canadian literary community."

If I'd known then what I know now, I would have spent even more time at Hart House than I did when I was studying at University College back in the 1940s. At the time, I felt a bit guilty about the hours spent going to plays in the theatre, reading novels in the Library, playing basketball in the gymnasium, and shooting pool in the basement. They were hours in which I could have been studying, bettering myself, preparing myself for the real world and its businesslike concerns. I could even have gone to class.

Now I realize that "wasted" time is the most important aspect of a good university education. The novels I read in Hart House, none of which were on a course I took, opened my mind to worlds I had never contemplated. They introduced me to language I had never spoken and thoughts I had never thought.

It is fashionable these days to assume that the university is simply a training ground, a place to hone employment skills. This is an assumption I confront at every possible opportunity because I believe that the university can—and should—be more than that. It should prepare you not just for the job force, but for life outside the confines of work. The university helps shape the future doctor, lawyer, schoolteacher or engineer, to be sure, but it also shapes the future citizen, parent, community activist or volunteer.

I look back fondly on my Hart House experiences. Much of what I learned in class has long been forgotten. I've discovered that one of the most important skills I developed in my university years was a sense of intellectual curiosity, a love of learning for its own sake, and a fascination for the unbeaten path. Those traits were nourished in the creative environment of Hart House, and I am grateful to it.

But, come to think of it, since after thirty-odd years in the world of real estate I changed course dramatically and went into publishing, maybe those hours "wasted" in the Library were job training after all.

Avie Bennett

The most recent secretary, Agnes Cserhati, points out that over the past few years the Committee has set out to articulate more clearly the special place the Library has in the literary life of the university. Like its ceiling, decorated with elaborate plaster roundels of creatures, plants, and whimsical designs connected to form an intricate pattern by a series of vectors, the life behind the Library is like a game of "joining the dots." All the parts seem to add up to a whole. There is more to the Library than just a room full of pleasant books. What emerges is a marvellous picture of the literary and cultural consciousness in the university's soul.

There are many parts to the Library. It is a place where books are collected, stored, and conserved so that readers, for the pure love of reading, can drop by and transport themselves for a few hours from the demands of the academic world all around them. It is a venue where a special collection, dedicated "to Canadian literature in all its forms," is lovingly maintained, and a forum for literary culture where contemporary authors come to read their works to the future writers of the nation. It is a publisher which produces an annual collection of student writing from across the University of Toronto, The *Hart House Review*. It is a place where young wordsmiths are encouraged to learn their crafts through such gatherings as the Algonquin Square Table, and a place to dream and to test their work against that of their compatriots in the open readings of the Writuals Pubs or the annual Hart House Literary Contest. Participation is open to everyone. The system is guided by democratic meetings open to both students and senior members of the House—gatherings that are picture-perfect displays of *Roberts' Rules of Order* in action.

A glance over a quarter-century of minutes from the Library Committee's meetings tells a story of acquisitions, struggles against decay and theft, and shifting tastes. On a very fundamental level, there are annual discussions about what the Library should purchase for its readers. There was a hearty interest in poetry during the 1970s, a shift toward literary fiction and non-fiction in the 1980s, and an effort in the 1990s to create a specialized collection dedicated to Canadian literature and the many Canadian writers who have been guest readers in the Library's reading series. In 1991, for instance, the periodicals accommodated such diverse tastes as the *Utne Reader*, *Frank*, and the *Times Literary Supplement*. Broad appeal with particular attention to quality is the best way to describe what can be found on the Library's shelves. There have, however, been moments when the students on the Selection Committee pushed the envelope. In 1979, for instance, the Acquisitions Committee tried to obtain a subscription to the drug culture magazine, *High Times*, but the purchased issues never arrived. Instead, the Committee was greeted with a notice from the Toronto customs office informing them that the magazine had been deemed "immoral and indecent," and "therefore would be retained for destruction," a bureaucratic euphemism for censorship. The minutes from March 2, 1979, record the Committee's indignation: "The Secretary was directed to express the Committee's concern at the arbitrary nature of the customs action." There was no further note made in later minutes of what became of the action or the subscription. What should be remembered is that it was exam time and students had their priorities set; battles were rescheduled for more suitable times.

Students in their COTC uniforms in the Library, 1944

Michael Ondaatje (left) at the
International Poetry Festival, 1975

The Library has benefitted from the generosity of many visiting authors. Those invited to read at the Library usually either donate or sell signed copies of their works to the Library. These autographed copies will someday prove to be a treasure, not only for Hart House but for the university. The recent installation of a security system has prevented considerable shrinkage in the collection. What keeps it in fine working order, however, is pure unadulterated bibliophilia and hard work. Library Committee members routinely dedicate their Sunday afternoons to checking and reshelving, and once or twice a year, depending on the zeal of the students, there is the "Dust-Up," in which every volume is removed from the shelves and lovingly cleaned and inspected. Every effort is made to ensure that the books are preserved in top condition. Frail volumes are sent for repair, and the two fireplaces, including the large one flanked by the portraits of Vincent and Alice Massey that so impressed me that first day in the Library, are now cold hearths to ensure that the books are given their best chance to amuse and delight future generations. In the past year, as Patricia Grant has noted, a great deal of effort has been made to shift the collection's catalogue onto a computer as the electronic revolution creeps in silently through the cracks in the heavy oak doors. The curators of the collection, such as the current one, Joseph Desjardins, come from the Faculty of Information Studies and are as knowledgeable about the electronic world as they are about the world of books.

Occasionally, the holdings are culled of books that no longer seem to fit the direction of the collection or the available shelving space. No longer is the collection an amorphous, eclectic gathering under the "anything goes" banner. The new thrust toward fiction, poetry, and Canadian literature has made the Hart House Library one of the most enjoyable browsing libraries in the city. Recent deletions have included cookbooks, exercise books, how-to books and, during the 1980s, the transcripts of the Nuremberg Trials, which were removed to another location in the House. Somehow, the records of grisly atrocities and war crimes, as necessary as they are to the ongoing consciousness of literary and national culture, seemed out of keeping with the casually idyllic atmosphere of the collection. If the removal of the trial transcripts signalled anything it was that a special free and protected preserve must always be kept for the works of the creative imagination—a gesture that seemed to many on the Committee a fitting tribute to the fallen from the two world wars.

As a place where literary culture can thrive through open expression, the Library has served well as a forum for authors. The regular reading series has featured a host of major authors and a focus for campus literary activities. During the early 1980s, the Graduate English Association provided a regular stream of readers to the Library Committee, and in the 1990s the Library has teamed with the Creative Writing Program of the School of Continuing Studies and the University of Toronto Bookstore's successful reading series to provide top-notch literary entertainment and engaging evenings. There have also been haiku evenings, PEN Benefits, summer readings in the quad, and the announcement of the Governor General's Awards for Literature (in 1996). For the most part, however, the fame of the Library as a place where authors can come to share their works has been the result of the diligent efforts of Committee members.

The regular Library readings have been supplemented since 1997 with the surprisingly successful open-mike pub readings in the Writuals series, initiated by Patricia Grant and Agnes Cserhati. "The usual reading evenings were often limited to the writers and the voting members of the Committee," Grant notes. "There was nowhere, it seemed to me, that students who had joined the Library Committee because they were devoted to literature and who wanted to write could read. So we started this pub downstairs. We had the idea that there should be a headliner, so we began with novelist Russell Smith just after he published *How Insensitive*. I was worried we'd get all sorts of dreadful things or that people would go on for hours on the open stage, but it was a great success." Carleton Wilson, who has been an energetic presence in organizing many of the Library's recent literary activities, notes that the "Writuals have been slowly taking off. This is sort of an 'Open Stage' event. One evening eighteen people signed up—we couldn't fit them all in! So we added another 'Open Stage' event a week later." The energy that such readings demonstrate are a signal that the tradition and literary enthusiasm is alive and well at Hart House and that the torch is passed from one generation to the next.

The cover of the spring 1998 issue of the *Hart House Review*, featuring a sculpture by Jane Buyers, Hart House Permanent Collection

---

Perhaps the most memorable literary event ever held at the University of Toronto was hosted by the Library in 1975 when the House held the International Poetry Festival. In the years since, Harbourfront has eclipsed the university as a venue for readers, yet it has not managed to assemble for a single event a cast of poets as exceptional as those who read in 1975. The assembled readers included two future Nobel Prize winners for literature, Ireland's Seamus Heaney and Mexico's Octavio Paz, and ten Canadian Governor General's Award winners for poetry: Irving Layton, Nicole Brossard, Michel Deguy, Al Purdy, Michael Ondaatje, Anne Hébert, Dennis Lee, Earle Birney, Paulette Giles, and Margaret Atwood. Other readers included the outstanding Israeli poet Yehuda Amichai; Anthony Hecht, later poet laureate of the United States as poet-in-residence at the Library of Congress; Australians Peter Porter and A.D. Hope; Americans Robert Creeley and Diane Wakoski; Canadians Tom Wayman and bill bissett; Senegalese poet Senghor; and British poet D.J. Enright. Years later, after a reading I gave at the Poetry Society in London, Enright approached me. "I read in Toronto one winter," he said. "It was at the university in someone's house you have there."

In one of the greatest understatements in the history of Hart House, the final report of the minutes for 1975 acknowledges the successful festival with only a cryptic statement: "It would be trite to say anything further about this successful event." The festival and the enormous impact it must have had on the poetry scene in Toronto are largely unrecorded, though it appears to have made clear a key need in the city: to have a standing stage for readings that would attract not only a literate and active audience but the best international voices of contemporary writing.

The impact of the festival was likely not lost on members of the Library Committee even two years after the event. The Writer-in-Residence Festival of October 1977 attempted to recapture some of its energy and excitement. Rather

The Hart House Library Committee Announces

The Seventeenth Annual Hart House Literary Contest

First Prize $150
Second Prize $100
Third Prize $50

- Short Fiction Works of not more than 3000 words
- Contest Open to students and senior members of Hart House
- Stories to be submitted with entry forms to the Porters' Desk, Hart House by midnight February 1, 1999

Entry forms available at the Porters' Desk.

Winners to be announced in April 1999
Direct any inquiries to Patricia Grant, Program Advisor (978-5362)

HART HOUSE
UNIVERSITY OF TORONTO

The announcement of the 1999 Literary Contest

When I arrived at the University of Toronto in 1979, women had been allowed in Hart House for a scant seven years. Not knowing what it had been like in the dark ages when females had been barred from the house that Massey built, I took access for granted.

I even tried emulating some of the guys I used to see upstairs in the Library, blissfully asleep on one of the long red leather couches. I went there to read Moby Dick, the biggest book of my second-year English class.

I read and read and read. And I got sleepy. I timidly stretched my body to fill the expansive embrace of the leather couch I'd claimed. I watched a guy in front of me. He was lying on his back. A T-shirt covered his eyes and his mouth was wide open. He looked like an idiot. But at the moment I envied his lack of self-consciousness.

I too wanted to sleep. Badly. Yet each time I shut my eyes I felt vulnerable. I thought that people would look at me too. They would stare as I had just been staring. And what if I started to drool? It was too embarrassing to contemplate. So I wrenched myself back into a sitting position and continued my own battle with the white whale.

The fatigue didn't abate. And I realized that if I wanted to be one of the boys I'd have to do more than get tough. I'd have to learn how to hang loose. I noticed the guy opposite me hadn't moved. He looked so damned comfortable. If you can't beat them, join them, I thought with a resigned sigh. I slipped furtively down onto my back, put my book on my chest, and tightly shut my eyes. I woke up several hours later. And as far as I know, I didn't drool.

Deirdre Kelly

than celebrate a single genre or an international pantheon of writers, this two-day festival focused on those authors who had served the University of Toronto as writers-in-residence.

Participants included novelists W.O. Mitchell, Margaret Atwood, Josef Skvorecky, Jack Ludwig, and Adele Wiseman, poets John Newlove and Earle Birney, and the 1977 writer-in-residence, playwright Carol Bolt. The particularly Canadian character of the group was yet another indicator that the Library was gradually moving toward promoting Canadian literature, despite its declining status in the English curriculum during the 1970s and 1980s. Professor Sam Solecki, then editor of the *Canadian Forum*, and Eli Mandel, a poet and professor at York University, chaired the forums that took place during the day. The big events, however, were the evening readings and the receptions.

The festival was also my real introduction to the energies of the Hart House Library. That was the year I became the youngest editor of Canada's oldest literary journal, *Acta Victoriana*, and as editor of a campus magazine I was given free passes to all the events, including a reception in the lieutenant-governor's suite at Queen's Park thrown by Pauline McGibbon. The festival promised to be the kind of stylish event foretold by those portraits of the Masseys. I was also enthusiastic about attending because it was *Acta Victoriana*'s centennial and I thought it would be a good opportunity to nab new work from some of the Can-Lit superstars for the special issue I had planned.

I showed up at 4:00 P.M. in my best jacket and tie at the lieutenant-governor's suite and presented a gold-lettered invitation. The doors to the reception room opened to reveal a pantheon of Canadian literature. There was Robertson Davies huddled in a corner, deep in conversation with Northrop Frye, both with glasses of scotch in hand. Frye startled me. I had only seen him perched in mid-air above the dismal landscape in the background of his portrait in the Pratt Library. I cautiously moved forward and introduced myself as the editor of *Acta*. It is a tribute to the generosity of both men that I was eased into the conversation. Frye had been an editor of the journal during his undergraduate days and likely felt a bit of nostalgia when my gawky undergrad self interrupted what could have been an important moment in the nation's cultural development. Both men told me to drop by and see them. Frye became my mentor through my graduate years and Davies became a regular consultant on matters pertaining to myth, psychology, and the writing life during our numerous constitutionals along Philosopher's Walk.

About forty minutes into the party, a buzz went through the room. "Atwood is here!" an upper-classman announced as if a herald of glad tidings. In walked Margaret Atwood. I had only known her to that point through her poetry and novels. I had always pictured her as a Rubenesque "Earth Mother" in a large woolly sweater, the way she appeared on the cover of her first *Selected Poems*. Instead, there was a small, delicate woman in a long burgundy dress that seemed to reach from the white collar and antique gold pin at her throat all the way to the floor, and the outfit gave her the appearance of gliding rather than walking. Her skin was smooth and the colour of ivory, almost translucent, and she had a glow about her even with a serious expression on her face. She was soon surrounded by the adoring and I decided I would wait to speak with her.

By 5:15, a rumour had begun to circulate that the staff of the lieutenant-governor wanted to wrap things up in preparation for a formal dinner that was being thrown for the authors at Hart House. I was standing off by myself against a wall when a bearded man in a denim shirt and jeans called to me for help. He was propping up W.O. Mitchell who, through travel fatigue or other undisclosed reasons, had collapsed into a potted palm. The bearded man grabbed Mitchell under the arms and instructed me to take his feet. "We've got to move him to the cloakroom before the staff finds out." He slid a free hand out through Mitchell's armpit. "Hi, I'm John Newlove," he said. Years later, when I interviewed a much different Newlove in the offices of the Official Languages Bureau in Ottawa, I reminded him of how we had met over a famous author.

What is so surprising about the cartage of the individual in question, who at that moment seemed comatose, is that at 8:00 he stood up and gave one of the greatest literary speeches I have ever heard. Mitchell was deeply concerned about Canada's fate. Speaking off the top of his head with the gusto that was the hallmark of his storytelling, he gave an account of his boyhood in Florida, of having to memorize the Gettysburg Address, of Lincoln's toil and struggle over a document that few at the time thought important but that now bound the United States together into a passionately cohesive cultural consciousness. He concluded with a plea for the Canadian imagination: "I hope we find our Lincoln." The entire audience in the Great Hall rose to its feet and applauded for almost three minutes. Canada may or may not find its Lincoln, but, sadly, it will never find another W.O. Mitchell.

The second evening featured Atwood as the star reader. As she took the podium in the Great Hall, she leaned into the microphone and announced in a rather hoarse voice that she was suffering from a very bad case of the flu. "I'm still waiting for the tiny time pills to take effect," she added. After the readings had concluded that evening, the audience was invited to the Music Room upstairs for refreshments, courtesy of the warden. There, in a corner by herself, sat Margaret Atwood, an exile with the flu. I seized my opportunity to introduce myself, even though I had heard she could be a tough conversationalist. Instead, she was charming. She, too, had edited Acta as an undergraduate at Victoria College. She, too, had studied with Jay Macpherson. Atwood became animated and nostalgic about her days as an undergraduate, and instead of dismissing me she told me she would send me some poems for my journal, which she did. Over the years, whenever she saw my name associated with a project, she would write me a letter of encouragement, and that to a young author meant the world.

———

Events such as the Writers-in-Residence Festival and the regular readings held throughout the year at Hart House are important moments in campus life. The chance for student writers, critics, and readers to meet successful wordsmiths means more than just a brush with literary celebrity; the readings are a rare moment when the continuum of literature is realized, when one generation that has reached the awareness that is essential for both successful art and artistic survival is able to give a hand-up to the next group. The Hart House Library operates on the principle

Let me begin my story with its ending. The head of the Hart House Library Committee is presenting me with a thank-you present, a book. We are standing in the Library, and the book is in gratitude for a speech I have given. The head of the Committee says a few gracious words. But except for him and me and one other university official, the Library is empty, the chairs in the room unoccupied. Where is everybody? What has happened to the audience for my speech? Have I bored them into drifting out of the room?

The answer to the last question is, no. Here is what really happened that night.

It was in November 1982. I had just published a new book, called In Court, *about Canadian courtroom lawyers. The Hart House people invited me to talk about the book, and on the appointed evening, a good-sized audience turned up to hear what I had to say. They didn't hear much. I had prepared a nice little speech, but on this night I was no more than three or four minutes into the talk when I felt suddenly, inexplicably weak. "I think I'm going to faint," I said. And I did.*

I'm not sure to this day how long I lay unconscious on the Library floor. All I know is that when I came to, I found myself surrounded by

feet in a wide variety of shoes. There were ambulance attendant shoes, fireman shoes, police shoes, and campus cop shoes. All the guys in the shoes had responded to a 911 call. I couldn't help noticing that beyond the shoes the room was empty. Somebody had dismissed the audience while I was snoozing. Down on the floor, looking up past the shoes to the faces of the emergency people, I didn't feel ill or shaken or in the terrible grip of some sort of attack. I felt embarrassed. I muttered something about "incipient flu." I stood up. The 911 crew left, and in the silent, almost empty room, the head of the Library Committee thanked me for coming and handed me the book. I drove home.

I haven't fainted since that evening in 1982, but every time I rise to address a crowd of more than ten or twelve people, I flash back to the Hart House event and feel, just briefly, slightly woozy. Then I rally.

Jack Batten

that literature is not simply something that is learned, but something that is shared. A glance through the minutes of the Library Committee reveal that the Library has been a wonderful place of imaginative commerce where many great writers have read and shared their works. Nineteen-ninety-seven, for instance, featured science fiction writers Robert Sawyer and Phyllis Gotleib, novelists Jane Urquhart, Eric McCormack, Lawrence Hill, Nino Ricci, and Margaret Gibson, essayist John Ralston Saul, poets David Donnell, Richard Sanger, Ross Leckie, and A.F Moritz, a reading by the Trillium Awards short list of authors, a storytelling night, and a reading by student writers of the Creative Writing Program of the School of Continuing Studies in honour of Canada Book Day. In what signals a former student writer coming full circle, novelist Ray Robertson read from his first book, *Home Movies*.

As Robertson remembered from his undergraduate days, "the thing I recall most fondly about the Library was seeing Morley Callaghan read there just before he died. He said that during his undergraduate days, the University of Toronto being very conservative in its curriculum, Hart House was the only place where you could read current literature. Even the bookstores were conservative. Hart House was the only place you could find Fitzgerald and Hemingway. Callaghan would go there between his law classes to read who was hip. He said it was ironic that a year or two later he met Hemingway at the *Toronto Star* and was hanging out with him." Robertson, who was working on a degree in philosophy but who harboured a secret yearning to be a novelist, found in the Library a refuge from "the heavy-headed thinking that goes with philosophy. Reading philosophy was something you did at Robarts, bent over a hard table with your Leibnitz and your Kant. The only place on campus I found that was appropriate for reading literature, and not marking it up and highlighting it and making notes, was in one of those chairs in the window, with the snow falling past on a winter day."

Direct contact with authors, however, is only a single aspect of the ingredients that contribute to making a literary culture thrive. Young writers need more than just contact with authors or even a pleasant place to dream on a mid-term winter day; they need to be encouraged, and in this respect the Hart House Library has again answered the call. In 1983, the Library Committee established the Hart House Literary Contest. This first competition, which has become an annual feature of the campus literary culture, was won by a student from Trinity College who was described by one of the judges, Mavis Gallant, as a "shy young man." Not only did Rohinton Mistry win the 1983 Hart House Literary Contest, he repeated the feat and was prevented from winning a third time only by being named a judge. The runner-up for 1983 was Kerri Sakamoto, who has since, like Mistry, become another rising star among Canadian novelists and who also served as a judge for the Literary Contest in 1999.

In recent years, the winners of the fiction contest have had their work featured in the *Hart House Review*, a beautifully produced literary annual that has become a stalwart among the campus literary periodicals. Following the demise of the campus-wide *University of Toronto Review* in the late 1980s, there was a distinct need for a publication that would speak to the university as a whole, that would override college considerations and offer a representation for the broader community

of voices. The first issue was published in the spring of 1992 and was edited by
Alana Wilcox. Editors since have included Sandra Kasturi (1995), Carleton
Wilson (1996), Sandeep Persaud (1997), Shamshad Bee (1998), and Caroline Li
(1999). As a joint project of the Hart House Library Committee, the Art Committee, and the Camera Club, the *Hart House Review* is a useful pointer to how the
various artistic pursuits can work together under the democratic processes for
which Hart House is famous. Printed at Coach House Press on an elegant, creamy,
textured stock of chain-laid paper, the review has come to symbolize a unique
amalgamation of good taste, surprising contributions, and artistic enterprise. The
inclusion of the winning entries from both the fiction competition and the photography competition makes the review a fascinating barometer of student tastes.
The first review in 1992 featured the photography winner, Andrew Podneiks, who
has since become a noted sports historian and author of books on the Toronto
Maple Leafs. It also featured the fiction prize winner, Chris D'Iorio, and a third-
place story titled "Two Step" by a Victoria College student, Ray Robertson.
"It was the first recognition of my work," Robertson recalls. "I remember getting
the phone call when they told me someone was going to pay me money for a
piece of my fiction, and there was a dinner and a party and a reading. It was a
big moment. It made me feel like I wasn't writing in a vacuum entirely."

Recently, the need for writers to connect has taken a new twist, perhaps
because the University of Toronto needs a degree program in creative writing to
supplement the recently created non-credit program in writing at the School
of Continuing Studies. Under the auspices of the current chair of the Library
Committee, Professor A.F. Moritz of Victoria College, the Library started the
Algonquin Square Table, a workshop/discussion group modelled on New York's
famous Algonquin Round Table of the 1920s, albeit without the barbs and jabs
that Dorothy Parker made famous. The Library Committee has recognized that
not only must it display or publicize literature — it must also foster the creative
process whenever possible.

What cannot be forgotten in any discussion of the Library Committee is the
role that the chairs, such as Moritz, have played over the years. More than simply
directing the agenda and calling the meetings to order, they have been guides
and mentors to the numerous students who have gone on to become writers and
lifelong lovers of books. The list of past chairs includes fathers Madden and
McConica from St. Michael's College, former editor of the University of Toronto
Press Ian Montagnes, and professor and biographer Elspeth Cameron.

To be a student member of the Hart House Library Committee is to engage in
the keeping not only of a tradition but of a treasure. It is a learning experience
that has been felt by many students — among them future writers such as Mark
Kingwell, Bruce Whiteman, and David Manicom. Carleton Wilson, former secretary, editor of the Review, and organizer of the Library's reading series, and E.J.
Pratt Gold Medalist in poetry, says, "I've learned more about almost everything —
how to work with others, how to plan events, how to direct other members of
sub-committees, lead them, how to put out a magazine. I feel like I've learned

more about actual working relationships from the Library Committee than from taking classes. It's been a lot of fun."

For the majority of those students who come to the Hart House Library, the experience is that of a quiet search. At a reading in November 1998, writers Barry Callaghan and Austin Clarke, both University of Toronto alumni, paid tribute to that room where the books live and recalled all those winter days when they, too, watched the snows blow by the leaded windows and felt the warmth and comfort of the Library. Said Clarke, "I used to come here to fall asleep, and then one day I opened my eyes and opened them and opened them." Callaghan noted that "there are many ghosts here. My father, Morley, found the authors here who would set the direction of his life during the Twenties—Fitzgerald, Hemingway, the journey to Paris. It is a place where I came, as a young man, to sit and dream and think about things I didn't have to think about but wanted to. There are many ghosts here, and they're all having a damn good time." Literature and literary culture come from listening to ghosts, from straining to hear voices from the past that say, "Care for this. Acknowledge this. This is valuable."

Maybe those sophomoric scratchings I made on the day of that November blizzard in the 1970s when I needed a refuge from everything in my university life never amounted to anything. They didn't need to. There were other days and other ideas and much more that I had to learn. What I did learn that day was that the world is not all work, and that good ideas can come when I take time to relax and just listen to myself. The Hart House Library was a rare refuge where I learned to hear my own voice as it emerged from the noise and commotion of the university world, a world that would otherwise have swallowed me. What I heard coming from within me that day could have been heard anywhere, perhaps to be drowned out by a due date for an essay, the roar of a crowded cafeteria or the grinding facts of a lecture; but instead, it was fortunate enough to have come into the world in the hushed silence of a comfortable, pleasant, and living place where the imagination is loved and cared for.

The set for *The Knight of the Burning Pestle*, designed by Fred Coates, 1922

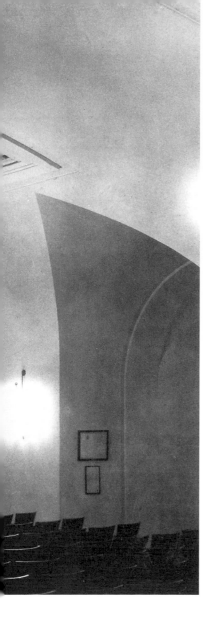

Chapter 6
Theatre: A Matter of Direction

Richard Partington

"This one's the very first production done here, *The Queen's Enemies*. That's Lloyd Bochner as a boy in *The Snow Maiden*. Here's *Mad World*—look, they're all dressed as insects. This is *Romeo and Juliet* in the '30s sometime, but I'm not sure who the actors were. Over here we have *The Devils* in 1967—can you see R.H. Thomson holding the cross on the left? And Charmion King in *St. Joan*, Bob Gill's first show here, 1947—isn't she beautiful? That's Kate Reid, of course…"

Jan Bessey, manager of Hart House Theatre, is conducting me on a personal tour of one of Toronto's most famous theatrical venues. She has worked here for thirty years, and it's hard not to detect her sense of pride in the place, her connectedness to every square inch of its physical being, to all its ghosts and memories. "It's a little steep," she remarks of the vaulted tunnel down which we slowly progress as she points to framed photographs on the walls. It feels oddly like the descent into some sort of Gothic subway station. "We'll have an elevator soon, they promise us, when Hart House's increased access program gets under way."

We proceed along a narrow corridor towards a darkened region which begins to flood with light when Jan flicks a few switches in an antique wooden box on the wall. "These switches are the originals, can you believe?" I follow her through a side arch into a bright space with a ceiling more generously vaulted than what we've so far passed through. I recognize the lobby from an old 1920s photograph I've seen, but it looks bigger somehow, less like the furnished baronial hallway of the photo. "We doubled its size in the 1968 renovations. This area was the former coat check." I survey the narrow confines of what was once the lobby. Five hundred-odd patrons would have swarmed through here on a sold-out night. How on earth did they manage a coat check here in the days of furs, heavy overcoats, hats, and galoshes? And with a bookstall selling all the latest plays? Not to mention in the mid-1930s, when the crowds were bellying up to Nancy Pyper's famous Sausage Bar. Jan points to a number of curious chrome slots set waist-high at intervals along the lobby walls. "Ashtrays," she declares as I poke at the layer of white sand contained in the bottom of one, "and right above each is a ventilation duct. No smoking allowed in the building anymore, though." She laughs. "But the ducts still work." I discern the merest tinge of regret in her voice.

We have come to the far end of the lobby, where a darkish mural occupies most of its arching niche. Figures disport themselves across a leafy, semi-tropical lattice of a landscape somehow reminiscent of a Pre-Raphaelite version of the Douanier Rousseau, the whole dominated by a magnificent shipwreck. "That's *The Tempest*. Fred Coates did it in the '20s all out of little pieces of lino." Of course, *The Tempest*. Shakespeare's magic and menace-filled romance has been mounted only twice in this theatre, so far as I can determine: once in 1922 during the Bertram Forsyth years, a production Coates designed, and then thirty-five years later in the Robert Gill era, a production notable for being one of the first acting forays of a young Maritimer named Donald Sutherland, in the role of Stephano the drunken butler.

Nothing has quite prepared me for the moment of entry into the theatre itself. It's not that it's a spectacular space—for that you'd have to seek out the Royal Alex or the Elgin, but they, after all, belong to a different league from this "little theatre," a commercial league—but it is an utterly unique space. With its vast, undecorated, low-vaulted ceiling, supported on either side by heavy Gothic buttresses, it looks for all the world like a theatre that thought it might also encompass abbey, crypt, and giant's wine cellar while it was about it. Yet, preposterous as these images might seem, while they all share the architectural imperatives of being underground—hence the vaults and buttresses—they also embrace the many-headed spirit of the art of theatre itself: its distant origins in religious rites, its wine-soaked festivals of Dionysus, its miraculous resurrections of the dead and gone, its potent evocations of both the real and the totally imaginary.

We drift down the gentle rake of the house. Too gentle, from what I understand. One on the list of the theatre's reputed shortcomings: no wings, no flies, no orchestra pit, and insufficient rake to the house, meaning by the latter theatre jargon that the slope of the floor where the people sit is not enough to avoid craning your neck to see past the tallest person in the world, who usually happens to be sitting in front of you.

Both Vincent and Alice Massey were amateur theatre enthusiasts, he an actor, she behind the scenes, in an era when the amateur "little theatres" were beginning to take the artistic and moral high ground over the corrupt and corrupting professional theatre that had been monopolized by touring companies from New York. Vincent's friend at the Arts and Letters Club, Roy Mitchell, would eventually write an extraordinary book called *Creative Theatre*, in which, while laying out the creative and spiritual ideals of this burgeoning "little theatre" movement, this concerted attempt to put art and community back into dramatic expression, he would devote its first sixty pages to an almost evangelical diatribe against the touring system that for years had stultified theatre into a venal excercise of 'bricks and mortar' and bums in seats. It was no accident that Massey invited Mitchell to be his little theatre's first artistic director. Some revisionists even suggest that the whole idea was Mitchell's to begin with.

Although I have many fond memories of my years at the University of Toronto, the ones that made the most lasting impression upon me had to do with Hart House. I happened to attend the university at a time (1950–1956) when the Hart House Theatre under Robert Gill was at its height. I was in seven of his plays. In those days there was virtually no professional theatre in Canada and the Hart House plays performed by undergraduates received national attention, perhaps not so much because of artistic merit but simply because they were the only game in town. The performers who trod the boards at Hart House were subsequently to read like a Who's Who of Canadian Theatre: Charmion King, Eric House, Donald Davis, Ted Followes, Barbara Hamilton, Donald Sutherland, Patrick Watson, Leon Major—and the list goes on and on.

Those were the days when the performing arts were not considered suitable to be taught at universities. Our theatre, imperfect as it was, therefore had significance perhaps far greater than it might have. I have always felt that one of the greatest mistakes the University of Toronto made in the 1960s was not to establish at that time a major Faculty for the Performing Arts, particularly when Toronto had become one of the great theatre cities in North America.

Hal Jackman

Invented by the Italians in the late sixteenth century, prosceniums were conceived as screens to hide stage machinery, lights, performers waiting in the wings
and so on, meanwhile providing a decorative frame for the stage picture. Later
centuries would come to treat the proscenium as demarcating the existence of an
invisible fourth wall through which to peer at the lives of the characters. Though
most prosceniums give the grand impression that they support the whole theatre
building itself, that is just another of those artful illusions which it is the job of
theatre to contrive. Hart House Theatre's proscenium is unique in being precisely
what it seems. If you tried to modify it in any significant way the whole east
terrace of the quadrangle would come crashing down onto the stage. Now clad
in wooden panelling the proscenium once boasted a simple but elegant 'Greek
square' motif as its plaster decoration, remnants of which survive in their original
state around the lighting and projection booths on the back wall of the house.

"The plasterwork's still there under the cladding, but it's suffered sadly over the
years from chronic water damage." Jan illustrates this with the amusing story of
an actor who, prostrate as the slain Laertes in a 1973 performance of *Hamlet*,
struggled mightily to suppress uncontrollable laughter during Hamlet's death scene
while water dripped down on his face from the leaky proscenium above.

She pats the stage in front of us. "This is six inches higher than it originally was.
They raised it in the major renovation of '66 when they expanded the apron."
Apron meaning a forestage—in this case a sizeable one extending fifteen feet
beyond the proscenium into the house. This explains why the proscenium now
looms at a midway point of the playing space where no reasonable proscenium
would ever presume to linger. Camouflaged in the same black paint as the stage
floor, it seems absurdly to be denying its immutable presence, asking us to forget
that it once stood proudly at what was then the front of the stage, an elegant
frame for the dramatic action and the stage design. Indeed, in its earliest days it
framed the scenic art of a group of men more commonly known for their bold
evocations of the Canadian outdoors, the Group of Seven.

Like Vincent Massey, the Group were members of the Arts and Letters Club
where, with Roy Mitchell as their theatrical guru, they introduced an uninitiated
Toronto to performances of commedia dell'arte, medieval mystery plays, and
such avant garde playwrights as Maurice Maeterlinck and W.B. Yeats. Mitchell
had no trouble attracting the Group to his new theatrical playground at Hart
House where, a technician as much as he was a director, he had designed and
supervised its technical installations. With Massey Foundation money behind him
he spared no expense in creating what Merrill Denison confidently deemed to be
"easily the most perfectly equipped little theatre in America." Denison, one of our
finest earlier playwrights, also worked as a designer and, along with Lawren
Harris, Arthur Lismer, and J.E.H. MacDonald, devised the sets and costumes for
many productions in the theatre's first few seasons. Denison's enthusiastic catalogue of the theatre's facilities in the *Canadian Bookman* perhaps best sums up, as
an insider's report, the enviable conditions under which they were working:

> Back stage the equipment is very elaborate... There are wind, thunder, rain
> and noise machines; carpenter, hardware and paint benches designed as

A production of *The Point of View*, by Canadian Marian Osborne, 1923.
From left to right: Vincent Massey, Basil Loughrane, Rauff de R. Acklom, Elizabeth Forgie.

interlocking units which may be used on stage for raised platforms, terraces, stair landings and so forth...all costumes can be designed and executed in the theatre workshops; all scenery, designed, built and painted on the stage; all properties manufactured there.

While such an equipment is enough to make any theatrical craftsman interested in experiment incoherent at the thought...it is the lighting equipment which is truly extraordinary. There are only two or three theatres in America with as complete or as large a stage switchboard. It has more than sixty switches with an elaborate system of interlocking dimmers by the use of which any group of lights or combination of lights may be controlled at will, dimmed gradually or rapidly, or fixed with any desired intensity of light... Almost any grouping, control and variety in color is possible. The lamp room is well stocked and includes large flood lights, spot and baby spot lights and troughs. There is a permanent cyclorama or sky cloth hung on rollers without which it would be impossible to obtain any feeling of depth or distance in outdoor settings.

Quaint now, but state-of-the-art eighty years ago. The emphasis on lighting virtuosity reflected Roy Mitchell's devotion to such European avant garde theorists as Edward Gordon Craig and Adolphe Appia, for whom lighting was the Grail of the future. The plays put on in the theatre's first decade represent a standard, though by no means uncontroversial art theatre repertoire of Shaw, Shakespeare, Ben Jonson, Euripides, and Ibsen interspersed with works by French, Danish, Spanish, Japanese, and—as befitted a theatre whose spiritual inspiration lay in Dublin's Abbey Theatre—Irish writers such as Synge, Lady Gregory, and W.B. Yeats. Yeats visited Toronto in 1920 and delivered from the Hart House stage a lecture entitled "A Theatre for the People" in which he praised the theatre and exhorted it to present plays that would not ordinarily be seen in Toronto. The Abbey, of course, with Yeats as one of its driving forces, had pioneered a national theatre for Ireland. Massey and his cohorts saw no reason not to adopt a similar mandate for this country which, at the time, was sadly lacking a body of home-grown dramatic literature. What the Group of Seven was doing for Canadian painting so Hart House Theatre would do for Canadian drama. To that end it became theatre policy to encourage indigenous playwrights by scheduling at least one or two productions of Canadian plays per season. By 1927 Massey was able to publish two volumes of the Canadian plays the theatre had so far produced. While it is clear from a perusal of these books that the dramaturgical equivalent of the Group of Seven was as yet waiting in the wings—alas, with the exception perhaps of Denison and, later, Robertson Davies it was not to make its grand entrance for almost forty years, and then not on the stage of Hart House Theatre—they represent promising attempts to express this country's unique spirit on its own dramatic terms, and we are indebted to Hart House Theatre's early practitioners for making what would turn out to be such a long-term investment. Later regimes would come to neglect this part of the portfolio.

———

Robert Gill acted in a Hart House production only once
when he replaced an actor in the role of Henry IV.

Curtain call for Moliere's *School for Wives*, 1956. Donald Sutherland is fourth from right.

Now standing on the stage, I look out across the seats and clap my hands, a rough way of judging a theatre's acoustics. The sound comes back to me with a bit of a ring, indicating a warm, full acoustic. "It's because the curved ceiling spreads the sound over the house. There's no echoey bounce." Paul Templin, production stage manager of the theatre, has joined us onstage. "Great acoustics here. But sound can get lost a bit upstage of the proscenium." As we stroll in that direction I am struck by how deep the stage actually is. "This is more or less a dual-purpose space now, with the extended apron. It works both as conventional pros and a thrust stage. Dancers love it because of the long diagonals. But that proscenium can be a lighting designer's nightmare. It gets in the way."

We've come to the wings, stage left, and into that region of the theatre where atmosphere, illusion, stage pictures, and the magic of lighting give way to pulleys, cables, counterweights, grids, scuffed scenery doors, dusty curtains, and unadorned brick walls—no concessions made to the upfront aesthetics, simply the gritty, unromantic mechanics of putting on a show. Time seems to have stopped circa 1935 in this area of Hart House Theatre. "We're a hemp house, you know. One of the last," says Jan. Sounds like some sort of opium den, but I do know what she means. Ropes, formerly made of hemp fibre, are still in use here instead of steel cables to hoist and suspend the scenery and lighting bars.

Jan counters the sense of arrested antiquity, however, by explaining that modern lighting controls were relocated to the booth at the back of the auditorium in the '60s, and that a spanking new sound console has just been installed house left on its own little platform. Paul points to a Wurlitzer-size object lurking in a distant corner of the seats. "Thirty-two channels in that thing. We get so many amplified bands here these days we've had to evolve to keep up. Even a sitar and tabla ensemble wants mikes. But it's a great room for amplified sound as well as acoustic." Roy Mitchell would turn over in his grave in envy at the possibilities of such technical wizardry. Then again, perhaps not.

Jan draws my attention to a tiny window above us among the cables and what-sits behind the proscenium. "The director could peek out from his office to make sure everything was going along nicely backstage." The director, ah yes. A bygone era. There is no director of Hart House Theatre anymore, no additions to the photo display in the foyer at the top of the ramp since 1979, nor is there likely to be in the foreseeable future.

To get to the director's office we walk up a narrow flight of stairs beyond the backstage area. I ponder this room's former inhabitants, the ghosts of whom suddenly crowd in with the present gentle clutter of a busy production stage manager. I peer through the little window as they must have done so often over the years. Roy Mitchell himself probably devised it with the architects; it's at a perfect height to view both the stage and the lighting instruments. American-born but raised and educated in Toronto, Mitchell had acquired his technical expertise in New York on Broadway and at the Greenwich Village Theater. Mystic and philosopher, like Lawren Harris he was drawn to theosophy. His productions were memorable, not surprisingly, for their progressive stagecraft, especially the stylized exploitation of light and colour. The most celebrated was his 1919 version of the medieval *Chester Mysteries*, a production with its origins in the Arts and Letters Club and staffed almost entirely by its members: all the male actors, design by Harris and MacDonald, and music by Healey Willan. Mitchell left after only two seasons, however, returning eventually to the more avant garde theatrical climate of New York.

His British successor, Bertram Forsyth, was more conventional a practitioner and considered to be, unlike Mitchell, an actor's rather than a technician's director. The former Oxonian had also achieved some success as an actor and playwright in England. Under Forsyth's four-year regime Hart House Theatre enjoyed a Golden Age which some say has never since been equalled. The repertoire was varied and brilliant, the productions well-rehearsed and admirably designed and the box-office brisk. Forsyth set up a summer school and an annual playwrighting contest and produced more full-length Canadian plays during his tenure than in any equivalent time-frame of the theatre's history. Hart House developed a national, even international reputation as a little theatre to be emulated, its success prompting the activities of campus and community groups across the country.

The skills of the non-professional actors trained by Forsyth blossomed to the point where some sought, and secured, professional employment in the prestigious acting worlds of New York, London, and Hollywood—Lorna Maclean, Wallace House, and Rauff de R. Acklom among them. Acklom, who died only last year, wisely changed his name to David Manners and enjoyed a six-year Hollywood career. He will forever be remembered as Jonathan Harker in the 1931 *Dracula*, starring Bela Lugosi. Most memorable, of course, is Vincent's younger brother, Raymond Massey, whose distinguished career on stage and screen needs no elaboration here. Of the many who stayed at home one can mention H.E. Hitchman, A.J. Rostance, Jane Mallett, and Ivor Lewis as among the finest. Vincent Massey himself, then a professor in the university's history department, trod the Hart House boards for Forsyth in such diverse roles as Pantaloon and Pope Pius VII. Mallett, described by one commentator as having a "matchless sense of the ridiculous," became the most beloved comedienne of her time. The smaller auditorium of Toronto's St. Lawrence Centre is named in her honour. Ivor Lewis was a versatile character actor who, in the course of juggling a day job as an executive in the creative department of Eaton's, also happens to have sculpted the seated statue of Timothy Eaton that broods over the main store's entryway.

Aloof and demanding at times, but urbanely witty, the charismatic Bertram Forsyth earned the loyalty and affection of his friends and colleagues, a fact nowhere more evident than in their expressions of regret at his untimely death in 1927, two years after his resignation from the theatre. Out of work in New York and clinically depressed, Forsyth, forty-four, gassed himself in the kitchen of his apartment, leaving behind a wife and three-year-old son.

Walter Sinclair arrived from a respected amateur theatre in Hong Kong to take over the reins, flush with recent international recognition for his meticulously crafted models of set designs. Possibly hoping to pay down the deficit of Forsyth's final season (though some saw it as an attempt to swamp the rival but ultimately ill-fated company Forsyth had set up after his departure from Hart House), the theatre scheduled a punishing season of sixteen productions. Resources were strained, quality suffered, and subscriptions dropped. Sinclair wisely cut back for his next season but, in his short tenure, controversy arose as to whether the

John Browne and Alexander Leggatt in *Marsh Hay*, by Merrill Denison. The 1974 production was directed by Richard Plant.

theatre's true amateur status was being compromised. And although he was able to do what his predecessors could not—remain on cordial terms with a somewhat meddlesome Vincent Massey—he left in 1927 for a more congenial directorship in New Orleans.

Carroll Aikins's rather kitschy three-act poetic drama of native love, intrigue, and sacrifice, *The God of Gods*, had been produced to some acclaim in Birmingham and, in 1922, at Hart House Theatre. The young Canadian had also pioneered the little theatre movement out west where, for a couple of summers in the early 1920s, he presented plays in a theatre he had erected on his fruit ranch in the Okanagan. A crash in the fruit market put an end to that, but by 1927 he found himself director of Canada's pre-eminent art theatre. A charming man, he was a dreamer with worthy aspirations for Canadian playwrighting—he produced Merrill Denison's Contract in 1929—and for increasing student involvement in Hart House Theatre. But over the course of two seasons he apparently lost interest in the job, declined to renew his contract, and never managed a theatre again.

Edgar Stone, active at the theatre since Bertram Forsyth's era, both as an actor and as a director of student shows, inherited the director's job merely as a stop-gap measure, and stayed for five years. During his directorship major excavations were undertaken beneath the Tuck Shop and the Great Hall kitchens to enlarge the backstage rehearsal and storage facilities. His regime was remarkable for the presentation of such daunting epics as *Peer Gynt* and Goethe's *Faust* and for an unusual preponderance of children's shows, among them *The Wizard of Oz* and *Peter Pan*, no mean epics themselves. He increased student participation—with giant shows like these he had to—and helped set up an experimental group, in part for developing Canadian works. During this era a children's company, the much-loved Toronto Children Players, emerged under the direction of Vincent Massey's cousin Dorothy Goulding. And in 1933 Hart House Theatre hosted the first annual festival of the Central Ontario Drama League, which Stone had organized as the local wing of the newly-founded Dominion Drama Festival. This annual, country-wide amateur theatre competition of which Vincent Massey was an instigator and life-long patron would come to have significant influence on Canadian theatre over its many years of existence.

When Nancy Pyper came to the helm in 1935, the Londonderry-born, British-trained actor-director-journalist from Winnipeg brought a welcome injection of new ideas and energy to a mid-Depression Hart House Theatre: "Toronto is to talk; Toronto is to laugh; Toronto is to forget itself...even if we have to put something in the sausages." Her mischievous remark referred to the "continental" Sausage Bar she set up in the lobby as part of her campaign to democratize the theatre's image of artsy elitism. ("Bring your own Mustard and Pretzels," suggested the copy in the program.) She put the noses of the old-guard acting crowd out of joint by using many new performers, among them her protégée Judith Evelyn who, after narrowly missing wartime death on the torpedoed ship Athenia, went on to Broadway fame with Vincent Price in *Angel Street* and an appearance as Miss Lonelyhearts in the Hitchcock film *Rear Window*. Her shipboard companion, fellow Hart House actor Andrew Allan, also survived the wreck to become Canada's most celebrated producer of radio drama.

Finally I'd arrived. Robert Gill had offered me the part of the "Waiter" in Tennessee Williams's Camino Real.

Needless to say, I was thrilled. Even if the part didn't have any lines, I was sure that I could do something with it. After all, this was Hart House. Everyone in Toronto came to Hart House, I had been told. Soon all of Canada would hear about the "Waiter" in Camino Real. *From then on it would be but a small step to Broadway, and then fame and fortune. I could hardly wait to begin. The following week at rehearsals, I got to meet the cast, all of them already legends on campus, with names like Jamie Mainprize and Jamie Cunningham. These actors were madly sophisticated to my eighteen-year-old eyes. I started playing my role with relish.*

But like poor old Penocchio, I too fell victim to the enticements of a fox and a cat. They came in the form of a couple of bridge players at Victoria College who persuaded me to have a drink with them one night before the show. I hesitate to add that I was a one-beer drunk in those days. After two draughts at the KCR (the King Cole Room at the Park Plaza, for the uninitiated), I turned into a staggering drunk, and tripped and stumbled all

Rousing productions of Kaufman and Hart's *Once in a Lifetime* and *Merrily We Roll Along*, a Victorian melodrama, and some fine serious works characterized Pyper's populist programming, and she endeavoured to make the theatre more available to the students. After her resignation in 1937, however, despite her two-year attempt to revitalize it, Hart House Theatre slumped directorless into a rental operation which persisted until after the war. Following a stint as drama critic for *Saturday Night*, Pyper landed a plum job as a journalist for the *Toronto Telegram* accompanying the 1939 Royal Tour. Inveterate name-dropper that she was—she claimed intimacy with almost anybody famous—the job suited her perfectly. A brilliant platform speaker, she tirelessly promoted the Canadian war effort across the country, moving audiences to both laughter and tears, and recruited for the WRENs as director of their public relations program. She finished her boisterous career teaching drama for many years at Bishop Strachan School and died in Toronto in 1985 at the age of ninety-two.

At the mention of Nancy Pyper's name, Jan informs me that it was she who initiated the U of T Drama Festival at Hart House Theatre. "It lapsed in the '60s but started up again recently as a growing concern. Four nights of one-act plays put on by any college group that wants to. And now there's the annual U of T Dance Festival, which was mainly Paul Templin's idea to set up. Nineteen groups over two nights. Phew!" "There's always the annual student shows," puts in Paul, "*Daffydil*, *Dentantics*, *Skule Nite*, and so on that have been happening more or less since the beginning. A few big names have come out of them too. Norman Jewison produced the *Varsity Review* here when he was a student, and Wayne and Shuster perfected their licks with the *UC Follies* during the war when it was still a review-type show. Lorne Michaels, who produced and directed for the Follies in the '60s, modelled his *Saturday Night Live* on its format. The Follies now does regular musicals like *Guys and Dolls* for a two-week run. Annually, it's the biggest show on campus."

———

It is important to understand that the theatre was not part of the Massey Foundation's original gift to the university. An afterthought, it has always been separate from Hart House itself, run by a series of separate organizations: the Players' Club of the University of Toronto for its first year or so, then the Board of Syndics of Hart House Theatre until 1966, when the Graduate Centre for Study of Drama took over and, since 1986, by the Office of Space Management. Another point to remember is that the theatre had, until 1986 at least, a dual function: that of a producing house mounting a season of plays, and a rental house, generating revenue for the producing function by providing performance space for a diverse assortment of student, faculty, community, and visiting groups— plays, variety shows, concerts, lectures, and the like. Over the years its rental function has remained largely unchanged, but its producing function has metamorphosed, roughly, through four phases: a community theatre nestled within the university serving as an unofficial educational adjunct for the student body (1919–1937); an undergraduate student theatre operating as an extracurricular training school (1946–1966); a professional company operating as an official

the way down Philosopher's Walk to the theatre. The denizens of the Camino Real *may have had some personal torments to overcome, but this particular night their main problem was a drunken waiter who swooped on and off stage, careening up and down platforms with a tray of drinks; making all sorts of unexpected entrances and exits; drawing audible gasps from the audience, wine glasses nearly tipping over on a terrified Dame aux Camilles and an angry Casanova. It must have been a harrowing experience for all: the cast, the crew, and the audience. I remember it barely at all.*

It took four years for Robert Gill to invite me back. But I had learned my lesson well. To this day, in a career spanning almost forty years, I have never again had a drink before going on stage. Plenty after, mind you. But not a drop of the stuff ever touches my lips before a performance. I wonder if they teach that lesson so eloquently in acting school today.

Bruce Gray

adjunct to a graduate degree program (1967–1972); and a student theatre integrated into a graduate degree program (1972–1986).

―――――――

Robert Gill, the last of the ghosts surrounding me in the director's office—the remaining three directors still live, after all—claims a unique position among his peers. He not only is the one to have held the job the longest—and by a long shot, at twenty years—but also can be said to have fostered what would amount to the virtual breeding ground of Canada's modern professional theatre. The Carnegie Tech-trained actor-director didn't set out to accomplish this when he arrived from New York to take over the job in 1946, but it was quickly evident that conditions were propitious. As the postwar economy picked itself up, Canada saw an upsurge in national pride, and aspirations for national self-expression abounded in all quarters of the arts. Theatre was no exception. A lively radio drama scene at CBC and the efforts of proto-professionals such as Dora Mavor Moore had already begun to fuel a spirit of professionalization among Toronto practitioners. This mood was catching on among the youngsters.

On campus, the student body of a theatrical bent was enlivened by the presence of DVAs, older students who had seen action overseas in the civilian theatres as well as in the theatres of war. Gill's initial call to the students for a show of interest in a training program and an undergraduate theatre at Hart House triggered an avalanche of response. He had only to bring to bear his genius for teaching, his uncanny instinct for talent, and his ability to inspire professional values in gifted but unruly students, and out of the crowd of enthusiasts who involved themselves in his productions emerged a generation of actors and directors who would soon help bring the nascent Canadian professional theatre to its feet. It has almost become a cliché of Canadian theatre history to list them: William Hutt, Charmion King, Don Harron, Eric House, Kate Reid, Ted Followes, David Gardner, Araby Lockhart, Barbara Hamilton, Henry Kaplan, George McCowan, Murray Davis, Donald Davis, Leon Major. Among the innumerable accomplishments of this remarkable Gill-inspired group, the two Davis brothers, who had first appeared as child actors on the Hart House stage, co-founded Toronto's Crest Theatre which, during the 1950s, along with the Stratford Festival, represented the vital core of the new Canadian theatre.

Others of this era of Hart House Theatre, such as Donald Sutherland and Arthur Hiller, would make their names in film south of the border; Fred Euringer went on to become a distinguished teacher-director himself at Queen's; Ronald Bryden achieved eminence as a drama critic in London, England, and as a dramaturge for the Royal Shakespeare Company; and none other than Hal Jackman, current chancellor of the university and former lieutenant governor of Ontario, claims to have learned his platform skills from Robert Gill.

More generally, Robert Gill's regime was characterized by his fine undergraduate productions—unlike his predecessors he used students almost exclusively—of Shaw, Shakespeare, and modern European and American classics. It is perhaps unfortunate, however, that out of almost eighty shows only two were Canadian-written, thus continuing a trend away from one of the theatre's early ideals. Illness and alcohol slowed Gill down in his later years. He died in 1974, somewhat prematurely, but not before witnessing yet another fundamental change in Hart House Theatre's history: the incursion of the Graduate Centre for Study of Drama.

By the mid-1960s, when it became increasingly apparent that both student attendance and Gill's directorship were in a state of decline, U of T president Claude Bissell advanced the idea of integrating the theatre into the university as a "laboratory adjunct" to an academic research program. The idea caught on and by 1966 official senate approval was granted for the new drama centre, with professors Clifford Leech and Robertson Davies responsible for its organization. After forty-five years in charge, the Board of Syndics was dissolved, ceding the management of Hart House Theatre to the centre. Davies, whose play *Fortune My Foe* Gill had mounted in 1949—he was a playwright long before he became a brilliant novelist—stayed on for a while as associate director, with Leech as the interim director, and in 1967 Leon Major, a former protégé of Gill's, assumed the position of artistic director.

Major, who began his career directing for the Davises' Crest Theatre in the 1950s, had recently achieved national acclaim as founding artistic director of the Neptune Theatre in Halifax, a regional professional operation of high standing. Given Major's credentials, the centre decided to experiment with a more or less professional company as its training body. After two years, during which he directed such challenging works as Marlowe's *Edward II* and O'Neill's *Mourning Becomes Electra*, for which he brought the by-then internationally acclaimed Kate Reid back to her old turf to play the title role, Major left in 1970 to head the new St. Lawrence Centre company for the next ten years. He was made a Member of the Order of Canada in 1981, went to teach at the University of Maryland Opera School shortly thereafter, and was recently appointed artistic director of the Boston Lyric Opera. He reports that he acquired his passionate love for opera from his Hart House mentor Robert Gill who, alas, was never to put his own abiding passion into practice.

Major's successor, the Cambridge-educated Desmond Scott, continued using the professional company in productions of Beckett, Ibsen, and Pirandello, but it was evident, finally, that the students resented their minimal involvement in the process. Scott, an accomplished sculptor and documentary writer as well as director, cast his final show, Farquhar's *The Recruiting Officer*, entirely with students. With the advent of Martin Hunter's tenure the centre was to abandon its professional experiment for a more student-friendly arrangement.

Martin Hunter boasts a relationship with Hart House Theatre that reaches back almost fifty years, first appearing on its stage with the Toronto Children Players and then in Robert Gill productions during the mid-1950s. When he took over the directorship in 1972, then-academic director Anne Saddlemyer asked him to approach it as a student theatre, in a sense returning to the Robert Gill model. Hunter, while accommodating this reformed policy of the centre, was to return, in effect, to the community theatre model of the earliest decades of the theatre by bringing in non-professionals from outside the student body who had, nevertheless, connections with the university. True, he did employ a few young professional actors who have since gone on to make considerable names for themselves: Jackie

Burroughs, Robert Joy, R.H. Thomson, and Clare Coulter. And in the special "Sesqui Season" of 1977 he brought back such Hart House veterans as Charmion King and Eric House. Ultimately, however, Hunter was a firm believer in the necessity for student involvement in the work, especially as directors. During the seven seasons of drama centre management which remained after his withdrawal in 1979, an era that saw the elimination of the job of director at Hart House Theatre, student-directed shows became more frequent.

Hunter's regime is notable for his revival of one of the guiding ideals of the theatre's founders, to produce Canadian plays. He directed two by Robertson Davies — *Leaven of Malice* and *Pontiac and the Green Man* — and James Reaney's *The Killdeer*; Professor Richard Plant gave Merrill Denison's finest play, *Marsh Hay*, its first production ever in 1974.

"Did you know that Roy Mitchell locked Merrill Denison in this room to write *Brothers in Arms*?" Templin offers with a grin. The strong-minded Mitchell would certainly have been capable of doing something like that. It was to be Denison's first of many plays, possibly his most popular. Evoking a slice of Canadian backwoods life in a realistic manner unusual for the time, it has certainly been his most produced play, with over fifteen hundred performances by 1971, when Robert Christie directed its fiftieth-anniversary production here at the theatre. After a stint writing historical dramas for Tyrone Guthrie's radio series *The Romance of Canada* in the late 1920s, Denison was lured to the States, where he created many acclaimed historical and patriotic documentaries for CBS radio. He was, after all, born in Detroit.

The drama centre departed in 1986 for new premises, leaving Hart House Theatre under the control of the Office of Space Management, where it remains today. The centre had a recent rematch with the theatre, however, when it sponsored a spectacular production of *Macbeth*, directed by the phenomenal Québécois, Robert Lepage. As we descend the stairs and move toward the stage door, Jan Bessey and Paul Templin regale me with stories about the show, how Lepage stretched the production capabilities of the theatre to the limit with his lighting, sound, and smoke, and an unusual "shrinking stage" effect, how he transgendered all the roles, how he had the three witches perform hanging upside down, and so on. Again, I'm tempted to imagine what Roy Mitchell would have made of it.

My tour has come to an end. "Hart House Theatre is now essentially a community theatre for the University of Toronto," summarizes Templin as he leans on the heavy baronial door which lets me out into the sunshine of an unseasonably warm October day. "What gets done here either comes out of, or is projected toward, that community. And, except for a couple of quiet months in the summer, it's busy. Forty or fifty shows a year of all different kinds, and the seminars and lectures can bring the total up to a hundred. But we're a leasing house, not a producing house. Those days are over."

Are they over? And is Hart House Theatre as busy as it might be? There are a number of people who disagree. Some think that it could be much busier, and serving more appropriately the university community and the community at large, were the theatre to be officially integrated into the operations of Hart House itself. Current Hart House facilities are bursting at the seams. An accessible Hart House Theatre could both alleviate this problem and also provide further stimulus for the development of Hart House as a whole into a truly exciting cultural centre. Besides, after eighty years of unnatural separation, the theatre would belong at last to the institution on which popular sentiment has always conferred ownership.

Others have proposed to restore Hart House Theatre to a producing role by making it the home of a permanent professional theatre company. Apart from its attractiveness as an evolution of the theatre's traditional mandate, and a consequent enrichment of the theatrical life of Toronto, this proposal would represent a valuable teaching adjunct to current drama programs at the university. After all, both Yale and Harvard boast residential companies. The reality of such a move at the moment, however, seems unfortunately remote, seductive though it may be to contemplate. To recapture the theatre's glory days with the wave of a new director's artistic wand could prove tricky in contemporary Toronto's competitive theatre world. Apart from crucial funding issues and the problems of regularly filling a five-hundred seat house for serious theatre these days, there are questions as to Hart House Theatre's viability as a fully functioning modern professional stage space, not to mention how to provide adequate stage-time for traditional rental occupants or address the banal issues of transit accessibility and parking. These ideas for the future, however, deserve serious exploration.

It is a fact worth celebrating that the ideals and aspirations of Vincent Massey and his colleagues have happily come to fruition. The progressive development over the last forty years of a vital indigenous Canadian theatre, with its long-awaited, much-hoped-for boom in Canadian playwrighting, stands as a phenomenon to make a cultural nationalist's heart swell with pride. That this phenomenon has, in the long run, largely found its expression on stages other than Hart House Theatre can be attributed, perhaps, to the caprices of time, possibly to the indifference of the university itself. It is certainly a function of its declining pre-eminence as a producing venue. That has long since been lost to its variegated offspring—the Crest Theatre of the 1950s and '60s, the St. Lawrence Centre, and the smaller professional operations which came to their vigour in the early '70s, like the Tarragon, Passe Muraille, and Factory theatres and, more recently, well-situated rental venues such as Harbourfront's DuMaurier Theatre. We have seen, moreover, the fervent amateur ideals of its founders absorbed and superseded by a rise in the highly skilled, diverse, and dedicated professionalism of an art that has only begun to come of age in this country over the last two generations.

A certain measure of cultural myth-making is good for the soul of a culture historically short of its necessary myths, and Hart House Theatre's colourful and influential past accomplishments have served very well in this regard. The time has come, surely, to take the future by its proverbial horns, but if Hart House Theatre can't do that in this changeable world then let it rest on its past laurels, and nobody but the most niggardly of spirit will accuse it of a dereliction of duty.

Debate held on Thursday 14th November, 1957

Mr. George Kell being Speaker of the House and the Honourable John F. Kennedy,
Senator from Massachusetts being Honorary Visitor

Senator John F. Kennedy (sitting on the Speaker's left facing the viewer) in the House, 1957

Chapter 7

Debates: Academy and Agora

John Duffy

In theory, the University of Toronto should be "the Academy" and Toronto "the City." If Socrates were to turn up on Taddle Creek, however, he might be forgiven for viewing the university itself as "the City." Bound up in the necessary affairs. The university's worldly imperatives — fundraising, grantsmansip, competitive research, land-use planning, human resources, etc. — sometimes seem to tower over the spirit of liberal inquiry on which the Academy is to be based. Even within classrooms and lecture halls the demands of grades, tenure, and intellectual fashion can kill the free flow of ideas. The Academy becomes the City.

Hence the genius of Hart House. Its mission is to hollow out within the heart of a great university an intellectual and artistic free-fire zone. To create an ungoverned space, with no stakes and few rules, where the fellow-minded can give themselves expression bound only by the laws, and a dose of common decency. If the Hart House Debates Committee were to draft a mission statement, the document might read: to subject conventional wisdom to contested scrutiny.

To suggest, however, that a Hart House debate is some contemplative meditation on geometric forms is to draw the Platonic line rather too far. For if Hart House is generally the university's Academy, the Debates Room is also the House's agora. The theatricality of debating — the grandstanding, heckling, and posturing — often overwhelm even the most serious of resolutions. Undergraduate orators strain their voices to drown out the trading-floor hum of student life in the rear rows and out in the hall. Political factions jeer and heckle each other's champions. New faces make smashing debuts as established stars stumble and fall. The whole contradictory essence of student-ness — solemnity and impudence, endearing informality and insufferable pretense, street-smarts and book-learning, academy and agora — suffuses the House, and nowhere so brightly as in debates.

Debating is to an argument as boxing is to a brawl. A proposition is framed: for example, that this House supports capital punishment. Two proponents argue the affirmative, two the negative. The audience decides which side has carried the argument. Participants confine themselves within this form of play, so that a clear winner may be determined.

There are only a few rules that matter. These, however, serve to elevate a formal debate far above the run of public discourse. First, the proponents must develop an arguable case; obvious truisms are out, as are limp propositions that can't be proven one way or the other. This is a test many election platforms fail to meet. Second, the opposition must clash with the government's case. Simply agreeing or changing the subject results in loss, the adoption of which rule would prove fatal to most television interviews. Third, ad hominem argument is sharply discouraged. So much for talk radio.

In fact, the whole practice of debating runs counter to public speech as it is currently practised. This season, Canadians can tune into twenty-eight different television talk shows concerning current affairs. On precisely none of these will the viewer find a sustained, closely argued clash of ideas between mutually respectful opponents. Leaders' debates at election time are even worse. Handlers teach candidates to stick to a "message track"—two or three very simple ideas that are to be repeated again and again, no matter what the question or challenge. Candidates seek to create "defining moments" in which they pole-axe their opponent by directly attacking his or her credibility. Winners are decided by focus groups, generally on the basis of "likeability" or the "Who would you prefer to have a beer with?" factor. The only thing that comes close is a courtroom trial— the conduct of which is a popular career choice for student debaters. But a trial is to a debate as a wedding is to a date: a healthy impulse obscured by dry ritual and over-the-top clothing. Debates are more fun.

The game has two taproots, one lordly, the other somewhat folksy. The first is of course oratory, an art as old as the West itself. The formal contest of orators constitutes a grand tradition, from Platonic dialogues through medieval disputations to such classic confrontations as the Lincoln-Douglas debates of 1858 and 1960's Nixon-Kennedy showdown. The second tradition is popular. With the advent of mass culture and education in the mid-to-late nineteenth century, debating societies sprouted up as a form of bourgeois self-entertainment and improvement. The Chataucqua Societies that brought learning and culture to the American frontier sponsored debates, as did the men's clubs of the rising European bourgeoisie.

The bridge between these two traditions, and the model on which Hart House debating is built, is the world's most famous debating club, the Oxford Union. The Union began holding formal debates in the 1800s, with variable numbers of speakers arguing each side of the evening's proposition. The Oxford debate combines the formation of young talent with lofty oratory and ironic wit to produce an entertainment as classically English as the Restoration comedy.

Hart House—modelled in so many ways on the best of British education—is probably the premier venue for this type of debate in North America. For decades, the University of Toronto has dominated debate competition in Canada and been a perennial contender in U.S. and international tournaments. Hart House debaters are, quite simply, among the best in the world, sometimes even humbling their Oxford models in direct competition. Debating at Hart House is, therefore, a success story: the transplant and flowering of a mother-country tradition on the fertile ground of a young nation.

Wednesday, January 18, 1928, 8:00 P.M.
"Be It resolved that in the opinion of this House, the social and industrial system advocated by the Communist Party of Canada is not in the best interests of the people of the Dominion."

"The man they wanted to invite was secretary of the Canadian Communist Party, Jack Macdonald—'Moscow Jack'…There was considerable agitation to cancel the debate…My resignation," recalled former warden Burgon Bickersteth in a 1962 interview, "was demanded."

According to the *Mail and Empire*, the debate went ahead before a "double overflow" crowd. The first speaker "on the paper" was R.W. Finlayson (UC, '28), whose father, the Conservative minister of lands and forests, had walked over from Queen's Park to hear his son speak. "We thought that might be helpful," said Bickersteth. Finlayson went after communism in general, colouring a vast historical canvas with Progress on one side and Barbarism on the other. In Russia, he argued, "trial marriage" and atheism were common, and the "animal and primeval instincts" had begun to dominate. The closer society drew to the state of nature, he went on, the closer it was to communism. "We," he said, "are painting the world red with British justice; the communists are painting the world red with blood." Stormy applause.

Speaking for the Noes, Mr. Gringorten, also of UC, sought to push the burden of proof back onto the proponents. "Do present conditions warrant a change?" he asked. A gentleman of the House rose, demanding to know the nature of the red flag dangling from Gringorten's evening dress. With a flourish, the speaker unpocketed the red ensign flag of Canada! Cheers. Laughter. "Mr. Speaker, the capitalists seem to ignore the fact that hundreds of people are walking the streets tonight to stop you and me and ask for a dime to buy a cup of coffee." Under communism, "each worker will work as much as he likes." More cheers.

Mr. Jackson, an alumnus teaching at Cambridge, responded to the challenge. Canada is doing well, he argued, measured by national wealth and by its distribution. There are, on the other hand, sharp distinctions amongst classes in Russia: between communists and non-communists. Moreover, Jackson grandstanded, freedom of expression is unknown in Russia. "The greatest security in this country is to let a man say his say and blow off steam without making a martyr or a pseudomartyr of him. Truth is never well bolstered up by bayonets."

John Leith Counsel, KC, eponymously a Hamilton lawyer, wondered aloud that "democracy must be saved, but by whom?" Not, he argued bafflingly, by the communists. His rambling, if stylish discourse pointed out that "the present tendency is to crowd out man's finer feelings in the struggle for money. If you do not believe that, you will make a fine capitalist, but if you do, you will make a damn poor capitalist."

Jack Macdonald was called, apparently unimpressed by the case argued on his behalf. "I cannot approach the subject in any mood of levity," said the Marxist, launching into a twenty-minute speech that was, by all accounts, "overweighted with statistics and facts of every kind." Again misreading his audience, Moscow Jack asked rhetorically, "I suppose you think that it is the brains of graduates from the universities which have increased...wealth?" According to the next day's *Telegram*, "There was a roar of assent."

The vote went anti-communist: 342 to 180. "...We became in the twinkling of an eye," said Bickersteth, "the white-haired boys who had shown how sound at heart the undergraduate body was." The *Telegram* offered another view. "If the debate did not bear promise of a large supply of future parliamentarians, it at least suggested that this country is in no danger of running short of after-dinner speakers."

———

Debating is a sub-culture. It attracts people who are out of the ordinary to begin with, and immerses them in rituals and passions that often seem curious to outsiders.

Who debates? In North America, students do. This contrasts with Britain and Australia, where adult debating is a respectable pastime. Not that youth is excluded there; the Australian national tournament of 1984 was won by two undergraduates who beat out a senior barrister and the leader of a national trade union. But in Canada and the United States, debating is emphatically a student activity.

The sort of student attracted to debating varies. There are two basic types—the earnest and the eccentric. In the United States, the earnest have their own competitive league, and do not debate the eccentric. Thousands of American high-school and university students participate in "on topic" debate, arguing a single, dead-serious annual resolution mainly by rattling off fact after fact from a stack of $3'' \times 5''$ file cards. Their eccentric counterparts have a rival league for "parliamentary debate" in the international style used at Hart House and elsewhere. Topics vary. Argument is improvised. Humour counts.

At Hart House, as across Canada, the earnest and the eccentric styles are brought together, sometimes in the same debater. Leafing through the House's photographs of pre- and postwar debates, one certainly senses the dominance of the earnest type. Sober, clean-cut "leaders of tomorrow" stare at the camera with wide, serious eyes. More recent images show, of course, a wider range of hairstyles, ethnicities, and sexes. But one is struck as well by the new presence of more artistic types, period dressers, and permanent students alongside the straight-backed sons and daughters of those in the older pictures. Debaters still go to law schools in droves, but they also study theatre, appear on television, start fashion magazines. The core trait is love of performance, a penchant for showboating that often puts a debater at odds with his or her more restrained peers.

Hence the clubbiness and intensity of debating cliques. Lifelong friendships are common amongst debaters. They huddle together in the small bands, refugees from their own weirdness. They identify themselves to each other by "generation," defined for this purpose as a three-or-four-year period in which one actively debated. They drink together, sleep together, support, and sometimes marry one another. Twenty years on, they grouse about running a substantive case against a funnyman team and losing the house vote. They complain of being robbed of victory by a "civilian" debate judge who didn't understand the folkways of the tribe. They disrupt civilized dinner parties with narrow arguments and deliberately confrontational tactics. In courtrooms, studios, legislatures, marital spats, they carry the experience with them all their lives.

Thursday, November 14, 1957, 8:00 P.M.
"Has the United States failed in its responsibilities as world leader?"
Guest: John F. Kennedy, United States Senator from Massachusetts

"I personally agree with keeping women out of these things. It's a pleasure to be in a country where they cannot mix in everywhere."

Senator Kennedy, addressing the House

America's first political superstar was invited to participate in a debate as part of his 1957 visit to Canada. The "rumoured presidential aspirant" came to discuss his favourite public subject, U.S. foreign policy. In a portent of future historiography, his foreign policy views were upstaged by his effect on the university's women.

"It was argued," said writer Ian Montagnes, "that every member of the university should be able to hear a visitor of such importance, even that for this event Hart House should rent Convocation Hall. The warden replied that Senator Kennedy had not been invited to give a public speech." University women responded with outrage. Campus newspapers editorialized their support, attacking the antiquated gentlemen's club policies of Hart House. On the cold, rainy night of the debate, a score of female undergraduates picketed the building, chanting, "We want Kennedy."

Inside, a classic University College vs. St. Michael's clash occurred, with the Ayes led by Stephen ("Steve") Lewis (who, incidentally, supported the protesters). Lewis and his colleague, A.H. Low of the law school, took the United States to task, arguing less the immorality and more the ineffectiveness of U.S. policy. Low accused the Eisenhower administration of contravening "all the principles of leadership," vacillating "in the face of pressure," and acting poorly as "policeman, baby-sitter and bank of the world." Their opponents, P.P. Dembski and J.J. Coleman, dutifully rattled off the many collective security achievements forged by U.S. leadership, including NATO, the now-defunct SEATO, the Marshall Plan, and police action in Korea.

Lewis closed by focusing on Kennedy's principal foreign policy concern, U.S. leadership in the third world. He pointed to American racial tensions, arguing that the forced integration of high schools in Little Rock, Arkansas, was a serious blow to U.S. prestige in emerging countries.

Kennedy arose, addressed the matter of the picketers, and got on with his reply. He pointed out that, as a Democrat under a Republican administration, he too had his differences with the conduct of American policy. Yet Kennedy took issue with Lewis's characterization of Little Rock, viewing it as an imperfect but vital step forward. More broadly, the senator said that the United States tended more towards the "awkward" status quo in security arrangements, but that this was vastly preferable for all concerned to the communist alternative. The House supported Kennedy, barely, by a vote of 204 to 194.

By the time the senator spoke, the pickets had dispersed. It had also been agreed that the senator would give an open address at St. Mike's the next day. An intrepid *Varsity* reporter, female and anonymous, had dressed herself in trousers, a trench coat, and a "press"-tagged fedora to gain entry to the forbidden chamber. She appears to have fooled no one, but brought off her caper with sufficient élan to force her way through. Her memoir of the debate, published the next day, ends as follows: "Outside, the girls were no longer picketing. I was disappointed. I had meant to ask one of them for a date."

——————

Where have all the Scotsmen gone? Compare 1946's Committee roll with 1999's. Then, male Mc's and Mac's. Now, members of every imaginable ethnic and racial group.

And even before the broad ethnic diversity came the women. The great House controversy in the 1960s was the full admission of women, a subject of passionate debate as much in the Debates Room as in the building's corridors and gyms. "Integration" of Hart House debates was treated with the same seriousness, and many of the same strategies, as it was in Little Rock. On January 20, 1967, the Toronto Star reported, "Five pretty coeds staged a sit-in at a Hart House debate last night." The *Telegram* added, "To the cry of 'out, out, out', they marched into the room and took their seats."

The widening of the Hart House circle has been uneven in the small world of debates. Ethnocultural diversity took hold relatively swiftly and easily, bringing women into full participation less so. Much effort went into correcting this problem. Numerous debates on issues of sex were contested throughout the 1970s, '80s, and '90s. Nineteen-ninety-two saw a debate in which four female debaters argued the proposition that women had rejected feminism, with the Honourable Marion Boyd, later Ontario's first female attorney-general, present. Yet debating is still very much a boys' game. It prizes such masculine conversational traits as confrontation, while downgrading empathy, or even careful listening. Of course, many of the House's debaters, and many of its best, are women. Yet others choose to participate primarily behind the scenes, serving on the Committee, often in the leadership role of secretary, organizing the tournament, acting in the effacing role of speaker rather than seizing the floor for one side or the other.

Is this phenomenon one of exclusion or self-selection? It is difficult to say.

——————

Thursday, October 30, 1968, 8:00 P.M.
"The maintenance of law and order must be the prime concern of a civilized society."
Guest: Hon. A.A. Wishart, Attorney-General of Ontario

The year 1968 saw student power, the anti-Vietnam war movement, and all manner of protest at its full flood tide. That same year also witnessed the assassinations of Martin Luther King and Robert Kennedy, the massive May demonstrations in Paris, the ill-fated Prague Spring, and widespread rioting in America's cities. With the limits of peaceful dissent being approached and often breached, the House sought to crystallize in the Debates Room one of society's oldest and most enduring arguments, with Ontario's chief law officer present as guest.

J.W. Person of St. Mike's took the unpopular side of the resolution, but argued it appealingly by focusing on the lawlessness of the state. Speaking to a recent incident on everyone's mind—a weekend confrontation between anti-war protesters and police on Yonge Street—Person allowed that abuse of the state's law enforcement power was as dangerous as popular lawlessness. "Law," he argued, "must be used legally." Nonetheless, he argued, the rule of law must be prior to other forms of political expression, as it is on that basis that a free politics itself can exist. He broadened his attack with the fine Catholic flourishes of a St. Mike's debater, stating that "errors" would be made in the pursuit of society's evolution, but that "only through law can man rectify the errors of man."

The first opposing speaker, J. Yaeger, deftly drove the argument onto the terms of the resolution (an unstylish but often successful tactic), arguing that if a society achieves nothing but the maintenance of law and order, it has surely failed to meet the test of civilization. He depicted law and order as necessary, but not sufficient, conditions of the desirable society. Making the case for civil disobedience as a locomotive of change, he (perhaps awkwardly) asserted that such acts were "not lawbreaking," but merely "supporting a law not yet on the books."

The next two debaters supported their colleagues' respective arguments with a barrage of examples, each seeking to outdo the another in denunciations of Richard Nixon, the KGB, George Wallace, and the U.S. National Guard.

Attorney-General Wishart took the floor with the classically disarming remark that he was "happy to be here, especially because the office of the Attorney-General is usually so unpopular." Appreciative laughter was heard. Wishart sought to balance the need for rule of law argued by the Ayes with the imperative of social evolution countered by the Noes. We must examine the laws, he argued, but do so within the existing law. The alternative is "anarchy and tyranny. Then there is no peace, no security, no society."

Speaking directly to the weekend's demonstration, at which twenty-eight people had been arrested, Wishart asserted that it had been "not broken up" by police, "but diverted." He drew attention to the irony of using violent means of protest to support the cause of peace.

Perhaps Wishart was forgetting his office, or maybe just trying too hard to appeal to a hostile crowd, when he suggested that "perhaps the police were wrong" in arresting the twenty-eight. Reported the *Star*, "after the meeting, he said he

During the 1940s and early 1950s, I was active on one or two of the committees and in debates. I was one of those at SAC who pressed for the admission of women to Hart House, and I actually made such a motion and wrote to Vincent Massey about it. As I remember it, the reply was very cold.

Perhaps as a result of this activism, when Warden Burgon Bickersteth came back after the war and met me, he was sure that I was going to be a journalist! Journalists, it seems, were several notches down on his scale.

Graham Cotter

didn't want that comment taken seriously. He attributed it to the 'mental gymnastics' of the debate."

Wishart's kowtow didn't work. Public debates are often decided before they start. Still, it was with a relatively balanced vote of 115 to 91 that the resolution was defeated.

––––––––––––

For most Hart House debates enthusiasts, Debates Committee sessions are their first encounter with the formal conduct of a meeting. For many, it is their last. One has to look to a parliamentary committee, or the board of a great corporation, to find meetings run with so much careful attention to procedure. There are good reasons for this. Debaters are notorious for unleashing stadium-scaled rhetoric on drawing-room audiences. Thus, the challenge of chairing the Hart House Debates Committee has always been to turn several convention halls worth of energy to a useful purpose within the confined elegance of the Committees Room. The key to this is conducting Committee meetings in rigid adherence to Roberts' Rules of Order.

Such formality is, of course, at odds with the tenor of our times. The exaggerated deference of addressing the chair, the patient wait for one's turn on the speaker's list, and the general inadvisability of heckling or interruption can be terribly constraining for a young performer. Yet these strictures are themselves a fine and comforting part of the traditions of the House. They give ritual and rhythm to the often mundane business of booking the hall, lining up a guest, framing a resolution. They force habitual talkers to listen, or at least think. The participation of faculty and alumni on the Committee forces professional courtesy even as it broadens the mind.

It is a still moment in the anarchy of undergraduate life. To see a drift of dust-motes as the autumn sun slants in through the leaded windows of the Committees Room is to feel timelessly, definitively, in the womb of studenthood.

––––––––––––

Wednesday, November 14, 1985, 8:00 P.M.
"That the West should not divest its holdings in South Africa."
Guest: Mr. Glenn Babb, Ambassador to Canada from the Republic of South Africa

"I think it was unfortunate to have invited the ambassador," said Stephen Lewis, Canadian ambassador to the UN, when asked about the November 14 debate and ensuing uproar.

In 1985, the idea that the University of Toronto should drop from its investment portfolio any investments in South Africa had gained enormous currency among students. A well-founded abhorrence of the racist constitution and regime of apartheid-era South Africa fuelled an insistent demand for action. Several countries, many investment funds, even the Province of Ontario had divested or were about to divest their holdings there. Would the university join the parade? The administration wished to retain its financial flexibility, and the campus's growing conservative movement took up the issue as a casus belli with the theretofore ascendant campus left. The convictions raised by this issue were profound. They extended well beyond the ambit of the university. On November 14 at Hart House, before the apartheid regime's representative to Canada, they boiled over.

First up was Mr. J. Canning, then president of the St. Michael's College Student Society. Canning argued loudly against divestment. He asserted that the policy would not inflict the intended harm, and thus would have no effect. Instead, he spoke for "constructive engagement," a path of reform whereby foreign interests, including investors, would apply their leverage to dismantle aspects of apartheid within their span of control. The crowd's heckling and catcalls rose and fell, reaching a peak when Canning offered that western companies cannot hire indigenous South Africans because of their poor educational attainments.

Speaking against the resolution, and for divestment, Brian Burchell rose above the practical issue to the moral high ground. Divestment, he argued, was the only way the university community could express its repugnance with apartheid. He attacked the Ayes' policy of constructive engagement, saying it was not morally acceptable to treat with such a regime. Sanctions and divestment, he claimed, would clearly have a strong impact on South Africa's struggling economy.

John Hovland of UC spoke for the Ayes. Often raising his voice over the jeers of the crowd, he laid out in further detail the case for constructive engagement, asking the house to choose between a durable, reformist solution for South Africa and the anarchy he thought divestment tended to favour. Tellingly, he pointed out that the United States had applied sanctions to obnoxious states five times in this century, and in none of these cases had such policies achieved their desired effect. Sanctions, he said, entrench governments, rather than dislodging them. He also tweaked the Noes' moralizing, asking whether they would be as eager to dissociate themselves from a country that was a major exporter of oil.

Ron Balkisoon, from Scarborough College, concluded for the Noes. He said there was no evidence that Mr. Canning's investors were using their leverage to promote African aspirations within the republic. Indeed, he stated, much of the trade with the regime took such forms as U.S. automakers selling armoured vehicles to the government. He noted that the most affected parties, black South African leaders, were themselves calling for divestment and sanctions.

As the floor was opened for speeches, the dam of order which had been held by speaker Rick Martin began to crack. Several speakers attacked the invitation to the ambassador, making it clear that he would not be allowed to offer remarks. Others defended the right of Babb to have his say, arguing the sanctity of free speech at a university in a free nation. "Freedom of speech is just a lot of sanctimonious nonsense," said one graduate student. Divestment is the behaviour of "a Pontius Pilate," argued another.

Mr. Lennox Farrell, an African-Canadian community activist with no connection to the university, was nonetheless recognized by the chair. He took the floor, haranguing with mounting passion the ambassador, who sat stoically, arms folded, with his security guard. Farrell turned to the old Bible box on which sits the House mace—the symbol of the speaker's authority—hoisted the mace, and launched it towards Babb.

Babb dodged the blow as order collapsed. He was hustled from the mêlée, as the crowd dissolved into knots of pushing, shoving, screaming factions. For the only time in the House's history, the result ballot would read: "Debate disrupted no vote taken."

A debate in the 1970s

In addition to inviting distinguished guests to participate in debates, the Hart House Debates Committee hosts one of North America's principal debating competitions. The Hart House Invitational Debates Tournament has been one of the principal venues for American debaters, and a must-attend for Canadians. An October victory at Hart House often portends a national championship in the spring.

The highlight of the tournament is Friday night's show debate, conducted by House members "in costume," playing historical figures. The evening takes the familiar notion of inviting historical greats to a dinner party and turns it on its head with a ridiculous resolution and over-the-top performance. Viewers have been treated to Tomas de Torquemada debating Johann Gutenberg on the merits of the printing press, Batman on crime-fighting, St. Augustine explaining fifth-century Catholic family values, and Marilyn Monroe wondering why Mr. Kennedy hadn't brought her along when he visited the House in 1957.

In 1992, Hart House was honoured to host the World University Debating Championships, the summit of English-language debating. Teams from many countries attended the week-long competition, which was generously sponsored by the House, the university, and several corporate donors. The Russian teams, in particular, are said to have enjoyed themselves so much they refused to go home for several weeks following.

Hart House has both developed and imported debating talent for years, but it was only in the 1980s, when the Committee amalgamated with the University of Toronto Debating Union, that the House began sponsoring teams in competition. In this way, the House added to its proud record of public debates and tournaments the lustre of U of T's sterling competitive tradition, which has brought one world debating championship, one world second-place finish, two world public speaking wins, and too many national championships to mention, back to King's College Circle.

Svend Robinson in the House, 1998

Monday, October 19, 1970. 8:00 P.M.
Emergency Debate
"That the present situation in Canada does not justify the Government's use of the War Measures Act."
Guest: Professor C.B. Macpherson, University of Toronto, Department of Political Science

On October 16, 1970, the government of Canada invoked the War Measures Act in response to the kidnappings by Québec nationalist terrorists of Québec's labour minister, Pierre Laporte, and British trade commissioner James Cross. The

War Measures Act placed the country in a state of emergency, suspending civil liberties, including freedom of speech and assembly.

Claude Ryan, the distinguished Québec journalist, had earlier accepted an invitation to debate at Hart House. However, with the imposition of the War Measures Act and the crisis unfolding rapidly in Québec, he regretfully bowed out. The Debates Committee was faced with a dilemma. Cancelling the debate was certainly the easier course, not only from a logistical standpoint, but because the debate itself could be viewed as subversive by a government that was now in no way constrained from the ability to arrest and hold without trial anyone involved in such activity. In effect, the debate could be held only at considerable risk to its participants.

It was agreed that the debate should go forward. The Committee acted in the belief that the university community had a special duty to dissent from the suspension of basic freedoms. The resolution was carried by a vote of 189 to 89. However one feels about the October crisis, or the government's use of the War Measures Act, the courage of the Committee's decision cannot be doubted. It mattered. It was the academy's finest hour.

A co-ed event at Winter Carnival

Chapter 8
Athletics: Transforming Amateurism

Bruce Kidd

I came to the University of Toronto because of Hart House. When my track coach at Malvern Collegiate in Toronto's east end felt that he could not offer me any more help, he encouraged me to get in touch with Fred Foot, the university coach. So during my last three years of high school, after classes, I took the College streetcar to the campus to train with Fred and the U of T team. We ran at Varsity Stadium in the early fall, the indoor track at Hart House during the long, dark winter, and Riverdale Park in the spring, but Hart House was our base, and the House became my home. That was in 1958. I still see no reason to leave.

Running with Fred and the U of T students in Hart House in the late 1950s was simply exhilarating, broadening my horizons in a myriad of ways. The entire north wing was a vibrant high-performance centre, one of the most renowned in Canadian sport. In the smug, conservative Beach neighbourhood where I grew up, the height of athletic ambition was to win the city championship, but my new training partners set their sights on the world. Some of them had first-hand stories from the British Empire, Pan-American, and Olympic Games, radiating the confidence that comes from getting there.

In the locker room, they would point out the veterans of national and international championships in basketball, fencing, swimming, squash, water polo, and wrestling, regaling me with tales of their achievements. George Stulac and Bill Yorzyk were the tallest of these giants. George competed for Canada at three Olympic Games in two sports—basketball, swimming, and the decathlon—and his workouts were legendary. Bill was the defending Olympic butterfly champion, the only male U.S. gold medallist in swimming at the 1956 Games in Melbourne. While a medical student and coach at U of T, he continued to break records. We stood in awe of these men.

The spirit of the south wing was just as heady. If I arrived early, I'd study in the periodicals room, or try to, because the cornucopia of reading material, much of it in magazines I'd never heard of, would usually distract me. After workouts, we'd go to the Arbor Room for hot chocolate, and I'd sit on the edge of debates about books and politics (I remember getting home very late after a long argument about Bertrand Russell's *Why I Am Not a Christian*), and gossip about profs like Vincent Bladen and Marshall McLuhan, their royal commissions and pet theories. Occasionally someone would take me to a class, the Hart House debates or a performance in the theatre. At Malvern, by comparison, most of us were numb with boredom.

Training with the university team did wonders for my performances, and soon I was winning almost everything in sight. During the winter of 1960–61, while still in high school, I became a headliner on the U.S. indoor track circuit, racing in Boston, Chicago, Los Angeles, New York, and Milwaukee, and winning the U.S. three-mile championship at Madison Square Garden. When Harvard, Yale, and Princeton came to recruit me, promising athletic and intellectual riches that "the little backwater of Toronto, Canada, could never offer," as one recruiter put it, nothing that they showed me seemed to match what I had already experienced at Hart House. So I opted for U of T.

During my undergraduate years, I practically lived in the House, training in the north wing, eating and socializing in the Arbor Room and the Great Hall and at Warden Joe McCulley's smokers, reading and napping in the Library, and attending as many concerts and debates as I could fit in. It was in Hart House, or across the street at the office of the *Varsity* (then published in the basement of the Students' Administrative Council building), that I got the hottest tips for my track travels to the United States or abroad. The warden, in particular, went out of his way to ensure that I never left town without a list of the "best things to see," wherever it was we were competing. It made every trip an adventure.

On one particularly memorable weekend, Bill Crothers and I flew to London, qualified for our finals in the British indoor championships, then flew to Paris. We spent the next thirty-six hours following a walking tour of cathedrals, cafes, and street life—sights, sounds, and tastes we had never dreamed of—typed out for us by Larry Garber, then completing his first novel, *Tales from the Quarter*. The rushes of adrenalin from that adventure more than made up for lost sleep, and the next day at Wembley we both won our races in record times. In the evening, we had dinner with a British journalist who specialized in Eastern Europe, a meeting Professor Gordon Skilling had arranged. I drew heavily on his stories for the essay I completed on the flight home.

These are rose-coloured memories, to be sure, but other athletic alumni remember their experiences just as fondly. The late Supreme Court justice John Sopinka, who briefly held the Hart House record for the fifty-yard dash, and completed his law degree at U of T while playing professional football for the Montreal Alouettes, once told me that he turned down a scholarship to Queen's because someone there tried to discourage him from studying languages. What he liked about U of T, he said, was that no one cared what athletes studied as long as they had healthy intellectual appetites.

Few other top athletes of the day lived this way. I would often meet players from the Maple Leafs, then the reigning Stanley Cup champions, at athletic banquets

When I was at U of T from 1975 to 1979, there was only one place on campus where people could play squash. In a university where students then numbered about forty thousand, there were three (count 'em—three!) squash courts, which could only be booked in person starting at 7:30 a.m. the same day. The courts were in the basement of Hart House. To get to them, women had to walk through a men's change room. It wasn't the usual change room, maybe just a team change, but a men's change room nonetheless. Quite embarrassing on both sides!

Patti Kagawa

and public functions, and we would trade experiences. During the iron rule of Punch Imlach, stars like Bob Pulford, Billy Harris, and Carl Brewer had to study for their degrees in secret during the off-season. In recent years, training and competition in most of the Olympic sports have come to require a full-time commitment, so that most athletes stay on the margins of university life, completing their degrees after they retire from their sports. Even intercollegiate athletics have become so demanding that most students have little time for anything else.

But during its heyday as a high-performance centre, Hart House represented the best of Canadian amateurism. An ideology of middle-class masculinity, amateurism insisted that sports be a character-building stage in a young man's life that helped prepare him for a professional career. It resonated with the Oxbridge values with which Vincent Massey imbued the entire House, but with a distinctly Canadian flavour: it was ardently linked with the spirit of nation-building that grew out of Canadian sacrifices in the First World War. The amateur code sought to enforce the purpose of education and selfless play by prohibiting participants from receiving any financial benefits from their athletic labours. In sports like gymnastics, swimming, and track and field, where amateurism held sway until its abolition as a condition of Olympic eligibility in 1974, the code actually made that purpose possible, by limiting the amount of time and energy athletes put into their sports, usually to one workout a day.

I remember one long, heated debate over dinner after a meet in Edinburgh with British internationals Martin Hyman and Bruce Tulloh, both Oxbridge graduates. I was extolling the benefits of training twice a day, which I'd just started doing. Martin strenuously tried to talk me out of it, not because it would give me a leg up, he said, although that was what I thought at the time, but because it would eventually lead to full-time training and professionalism, and end the well-rounded life amateurism enabled. How prophetic Martin was!

The glory years of Hart House athletics coincided with and contributed to the golden age of amateurism in Canada. The University of Toronto Athletic Association, the volunteer body that governed male athletics in the university until the mid-1970s, when the Department of Athletics and Recreation was created and the Stevens Building opened, was one of its leading advocates in Canadian intercollegiate and Olympic sports. Most of the staff with whom students interacted, from athletic director Warren Stevens and his able assistant Phyllis Lea to the workers in the laundry room, expected students to combine sports with serious study and the other intellectual and cultural activities the university offered. For those of us who had the means to do so, Hart House made that expectation an engrossing reality.

The north wing was the university's fourth gymnasium (as it was first called) or fifth, if you count the Temporary Gymnasium, with its concrete swimming pool, which was put up on the Trinity Athletic Field during the years of construction on Hart House. When the athletic wing opened on November 11, 1919, it represented a significant advance over the previous building on the same site. The pool (75′ × 40′) was three times the size of the one it replaced, the new track twice as long, reducing the number of laps from 21 to 11.5 a mile. There were 5 well-equipped gymnasiums of various sizes.

Before women were admitted into the pool

The Hart House swimming pool has elegant vaulted arches, a skylight that ushers in wavering natural light, intricate white tiling, and aquamarine water that's a degree or two colder than most competitive pools. It's a sublime place to swim—to lose yourself in repetitive motion, to reach that buoyant physical high when your body becomes fluid and escapes all bounds. Back and forth, back and forth. Ten laps the first time you try. Twenty laps the next. In a month you've made seventy laps—a mile.

Once, in the mid-1980s, during the height of my obsession with swimming, I made five miles without stopping. Five more notches on the lap chart by the towel desk. Looking back, I'm incredulous when I estimate that I swam about two thousand miles in ten years.

Why? The answer lies beyond the predictable ones of well-being, obsessiveness, and competitiveness with friends who were also swimming. What sent me racing for enormous distances in the Hart House pool was the hair ball that resided at the bottom of the right lane at the far end. The hair ball was always there, in spite of the efforts of the lifeguards and the night maintenance crew. It was the size of a grapefruit, a hirsute macramé *that bobbed in the bottom corner, making occasional forays to the surface. The introduction of women and suits to the pool did nothing to deter the hair ball's resilience.*

The first time you saw the hair ball, you panicked, but sped up to try to avoid it. Each turn at the far end became a Homeric endeavour of courage — touch the wall before the monster of hair and soap scum got you in the face. My marathon in the Hart House pool was propelled by nothing more than terror of the glob nestled in the corner.

A few years ago Hart House listened to the myriad of complaints about the hair ball and took extreme measures. It installed a new filtration system and retiled the pool. The hair ball disappeared, but with it so did much of my desire to swim. I still try to do a mile a couple of times a week, but the adrenalin doesn't kick in the way it used to. Accomplishment just doesn't come without fear.

Ian Pearson

The new facilities gave male U of T students a tremendous boost. In 1920–21, the first full year of operation, they helped athletes win intercollegiate titles in basketball, boxing, fencing, gymnastics, and wrestling, every indoor sport then contested with the exception of water polo (which was won by McGill). U of T remained a powerhouse in indoor sports for decades. While there was no intercollegiate competition in squash until after the war, there were lots of other challenges, and the intensity of the ladder matches on the Hart House courts enabled U of T students to compete with the best. In 1954, Ernie Howard won the Canadian and American open championship.

The Hart House track helped several generations of students achieve world-class performances. Visitors today are amazed that anyone could seriously train on the track, let alone turn in the outstanding times recorded in the 1930s, 1950s, and 1960s. But for its time, it was a godsend: no one else in Canada had anything like it until the 1970s. The short straightaways limited its usefulness for sprinters, but for us middle-distance and distance runners it meant that we could do hard workouts in the dead of winter, without the fear of traffic, frozen feet, and falls on ice which our rivals in other Canadian clubs had to face. Moreover, it gave us an unexpected edge. The narrow width, the tight, high-banked corners, and the possibility that at any time someone might step out unexpectedly from the stairwell directly into your path sharpened our instincts (and our elbows!): we learned to thread our way through a crowd and run low on the turn at full speed. Competing on the wider, 160-yard U.S. tracks, U of T runners were rarely boxed in, and could often pass on the inside.

The one blemish was the main gym, which was kept to the same 100′ × 50′ dimensions of the nineteenth-century building. It meant that basketball had to be played on a smaller-than-regulation court, and even then, players ran the risk of slamming into a wall after running for a basket or if they stepped out of bounds. On the other hand, the "cage," as it came to be called, was discombobulating for opponents. One visiting American coach first took it as a compliment — "It's very hospitable of you to provide a crowd for the warm-up gym," he told U of T coach John McManus — until he realized that the game would be played there. He almost took his team back to the dressing room then and there.

While the small court put U of T teams at a disadvantage on the road, it gave them a tremendous home court advantage. During my undergraduate years, with guards like Peter "Rabbit" Potter and David West controlling the lanes, and Varsity fans screaming from every available nook and cranny, it was worth at least twenty points a game.

In this day of plush, commodious arenas and domed stadiums, it's hard to believe that for many years Hart House was a premier competition facility for men's sports, as well known as Varsity Stadium and Varsity Arena. During the winter months, "Varsity Athletic Nights," intercollegiate competitions in several sports, followed by dances, were held most weekends. Spectators could move freely from event to event. Except for the pool and the main gym, where there was limited seating, spectators stood, often pressed three and four rows deep into whatever space was available. For important basketball games, the bleachers on the gym floor would be full, fans would sit and stand on chairs placed along the track above, and, if there were no marshals, scrunch themselves into a vantage point on the spiral staircase that connected the first and second floors in the north-east corner of the gym, or on the steel rafters above the track. Crowds of nine hundred for swim meets and two thousand for basketball were not uncommon.

Hart House hosted not only university competitions, but also high-school, provincial, and national championships, and even international invitationals. In the 1950s and 1960s, for example, the swim team generated revenue by staging an annual Water Carnival, two evenings of swimming, water polo, diving, syn-chronized swimming, and aqua lung (scuba) competitions and exhibitions with a parade of invited Canadian and American stars. The 1959 carnival saw American backstroker Carin Cone equal her world record, and twenty-eight Canadian records were broken or tied. It attracted fourteen hundred paying spectators at $1.25 a ticket.

Amateurism also meant "athletics for all" — at least all men. The north wing enabled the UTAA to expand intramural and instructional programs, so that all male students could participate. Prior to World War One, colleges and faculties had competed in basketball, boxing, fencing, water polo, and wrestling. Once the House was opened, interfaculty competitions were added in indoor baseball, box lacrosse, gymnastics, swimming, and track and field. By 1931–32, under the gifted administration of John McCutcheon, there were ninety-seven teams compet-ing in thirteen sports (including football, ice hockey, soccer, and tennis played elsewhere). Total participation represented 66 percent of the male student body.

Still, students wanted more. In 1937, at the instigation of SAC, the university agreed to impose a $3.00 fee on all students, in return for opening the north wing in the evenings (previously, it had been closed at 6:00), providing students with free admission to all men's intercollegiate football and hockey games, and to Varsity Stadium. The university also provided instruction in figure skating and golf, and "accommodation for skiing within a reasonable distance from Toronto," an annual grant to the Women's Athletic Association, and "the maintenance of an emergency surgical service and an attendant at intramural games to cover any accidents that may occur." (Medical care for intercollegiate games was introduced at U of T in 1906. SAC's initiative led to the opening of a small surgery in the base-ment of the athletic wing. Today the David L. MacIntosh Sports Medicine Clinic — named after the physician who operated it for many years — in the Athletic and Physical Education Centre is the oldest continuously operating service of its kind in North America.)

Such was the origin of the compulsory athletic fee.

In the years that followed, competitions were added in badminton, squash, and volleyball, and, outdoors, golf and rugby. Right up until the late 1970s, some of the intramural championships were as closely followed as the intercollegiates. I can remember scrambling unsuccessfully to find a place to stand for one Dafoe Cup box lacrosse final between students in law and physical and health education. The place was packed to the rafters.

For decades male undergraduates who were not otherwise active in intercolle-giate or intramural sports were required to take two years of physical education classes in Hart House conducted by the Department of Physical Education (Men).

The most important requirement was that students learn to swim. It actually became a prerequisite for graduation. For many years the need was so great that instructional classes were provided on an hourly basis throughout the day. For those who wanted to continue beyond the basic test, advanced courses in swimming and diving were provided, and students could earn certification from the Royal Life Saving Society of Canada. As a result, thousands of students became competent in the water. Hundreds more obtained RLSS qualifications, standing them in good stead in the summer job market, where lifeguard and waterfront leadership positions in municipal recreation and summer camps were among the best paid.

Physical education classes in the gyms were less successful, however, especially in the crowded classes after World War Two. Instruction was rigid, repetitive, and unimaginative. Uniforms (white T-shirts, blue shorts) were compulsory. Each student was given a tight square to stand and move in, set out by a mark on the floor. A monitor walking along the track above took attendance. The instructor stood on a platform, barking out drills in boxing, calisthenics or gymnastics. A photograph of a typical class in the 1940s shows the entire floor of the main gym filled with rows of male student boxers in exactly the same pose. This alienating approach no doubt taught many to hate physical education, and may have turned them away from a lifestyle of physical activity. Pressure of numbers forced the university to drop the second year of compulsory physical education for men in 1952, and eliminate the requirement entirely in 1968.

By the late 1960s, the winds of change were blowing at gale force. It was not only the dramatic increase in enrolment that made it abundantly clear that Hart House could no longer adequately serve the student population, rekindling long-held hopes for a new athletic building. The counter-culture the baby boomers brought to the university scorned the ideals of competition on which the athletic culture of the House rested, arguing that it reinforced elitism, sexism, and the militarism then out of control in southeast Asia. This critique, voiced by a succession of articulate Varsity sports editors and student political leaders, no doubt contributed to the decision to eliminate compulsory physical education. As an alternative, the critics called for more casual recreation, co-operative games, and fitness activities in which everyone could set his or her own goals. These aspirations spurred the rebirth of the fitness movement under a more hedonistic guise. They contributed in important ways to the future of the north wing.

The youth radicalization also fuelled the women's liberation movement's challenge to the male monopoly of the House. It was a source of bitterness to all women's groups on campus, but athletic women were particularly aggrieved. They had been promised their own building at the time Hart House opened, but it would take another forty years of constant prodding before they could get the university to deliver, with the Benson Building, in 1959. Until then, women were forced to use a number of inferior facilities on and off campus.

On occasion, as we have seen, the facilities at Hart House had been made available for women's competition. The swim and track teams were often supportive, staging women's races and exhibitions in their invitational events. But these crumbs only fanned the fire. Women took advantage of every opportunity to sneak into

Senior Members' Sports Night in the gym

Abby Hoffman and Bruce Kidd, c.1980

the north wing, sometimes passing as men, sometimes assisted by men (as runners like Marion Munroe Snider did in my generation), sometimes completely on their own. Oh, for a full oral history of such escapades! Of those I've heard, my favourite comes from the 1920s. During a guided tour of Hart House, Helen Bryans and a friend were admiring the deserted swimming pool when the rest of their group wandered off, leaving them alone. Bryans, who later became senior professor of physical education at the Ontario College of Education, quickly locked the door, stripped off her clothes, swam two lengths in the patriarchy's inner sanctum, climbed out, and gave a cheer.

It was Abby Hoffman, the four-time Canadian Olympian, who turned the long-simmering discontent into a battle cry. Unprepared to wait for the few opportunities available, or to masquerade as a man, Abby challenged the male monopoly head on. During the winter of 1966, she tried to use the track on three separate occasions, only to be forcefully ejected from the building each time. A year later, the UTAA added insult to injury. After agreeing to contribute to the expenses of all U of T athletes in the World University Games, it sent Abby a bill for her portion of the costs, on the grounds that as a female she was "not an athletic member." One of Canada's most articulate sports leaders, Abby was quick to publicize her mistreatment, adding considerably to the rising chorus calling for full integration.

The admission of women into the House in 1972 and the general spread of second-wave feminism forced us men to reappraise what we had once taken for granted. The disruption of the familiar rhythms of the north wing the women caused (such as "forcing" us to wear bathing suits in the pool) and their often sharp observations of the culture they encountered brought home how privileged we men had been. If democratic access to higher education was ever to be achieved, it became clear, then the opportunities for physical self-mastery, culture, and companionship that we had enjoyed needed to be just as available to women.

The integration of the north wing also served to strip away the received male notion of the "naturalness" of competitive sports, revealing a profoundly masculine system of cultural expression. The policy implications of this awareness are much more complicated. On the one hand, sports are closely bound up with the system that gives men power in modern societies, setting an important standard for social status and acclaim against which women—who have fewer opportunities—are usually found wanting. It is not only the tremendous investments in male sports alongside the history of prohibitions against women that give men such a clear field, but the very ambiance of sports. It was during the 1970s that I first discovered how foreboding the athletic wing of the House was to many women, with its fortress-like exterior, trench-like underground corridors, unkempt brick walls, and dark corners. The fierce competitive spirit that reigned within was no more welcoming.

For these reasons, most women continued to rely upon the Benson Building, as before. The greatest deterrent was the lack of adequate changing and showering rooms for women. It was only in 1979, after several false starts and much lobbying, that a small room with showers was provided in what had been the graduate men's changing room. Abby Hoffman graciously agreed to cut the official ribbon.

The plaque commemorating the opening quoted Nelly McClung: "Only she who attempts the absurd can achieve the impossible."

But other changes would accelerate the transformation of the north wing. In 1974, the university decided to amalgamate the governance and administration of men's and women's athletics and physical education and to construct the New Athletic Building (NAB) adjacent to the Benson Building so that there could be an integrated Athletic and Physical Education Centre (AC). All Hart House activities would be moved into the new AC. The UTAA, the Department of Physical Education (Men), the Women's Athletic Association, and the Department of Physical Education (Women) were to be merged into the Department of Athletics and Recreation (DAR). DAR began operations in 1977. The NAB, eventually named after long-serving men's athletic director Warren Stevens, was opened in 1979.

While others had their eye on the north wing, the university agreed to continue its use for athletics for a five-year trial period under the direction of the Board of Stewards. The committees struck to recommend future use proposed that it focus on activities that would be co-educational, unstructured, and complementary to the NAB. When the DAR vacated Hart House in the summer of 1979, taking most of the equipment with it, the Board of Stewards created the Recreational Athletics Committee to oversee the north wing. The Committee hired W.A.B. "Sandy" Henderson to serve as recreation officer. Sandy quickly put in place an extensive program of instructional classes in fitness and dance, introduced a new system of squash court reservations, and purchased new equipment. The pool, track, and most court times were reserved for open recreation.

The transition to non-competitive activities proved smoother than most had expected. The fitness boom was in full swing, and hundreds of avid new lap swimmers and joggers happily discovered the unprogrammed facilities. It was clear that the new AC could not serve all the needs of U of T's still-growing population, especially those students, faculty, and staff on the east campus who did not always have the time to trek all the way across to Harbord and Spadina. Moreover, most alumnae and alumni chose to stay with Hart House. In 1981, just two years after the trial was begun, the university brought it to an end, declaring that the north wing would remain an athletic facility for the foreseeable future.

Of course, there were growing pains. The weight-room culture remained hostile to women for many years. In some cases, basketball players took licence from "open recreation" to control courts for long periods of time. These practices forced Sandy and his staff to intervene. But in most cases, the participants sorted out issues themselves.

For example, the increasing popularity of aerobics classes in the main gym, with speakers blasting out popular music, infuriated those accustomed to a quiet, reflective run around the track above. It mattered little that many senior members had been attracted back to the House by the pioneering fitness classes begun more than a decade earlier by Professor Juri Daniel. For a painfully protracted period in the early 1980s, disagreements about aesthetics and noise levels often touched off shouting matches between runners and fitness participants, ensuring a steady, heated correspondence between members and the Recreation Committee. It took the diplomacy of instructor Iris Weller to repair the damage. Recognizing that one of her professors, Sherwin Desser, was among the aggrieved noonday running group, she asked him what music to play. "Chariots of Fire" was the reply. It seemed to work.

Competitive sports have not disappeared entirely from the House. Although the U of T team no longer uses the track, men and women still train to race, and there's an open time trial every Friday afternoon. During the 1970s and 1980s, John Reeves organized an annual 26-mile marathon — 301.5 laps of continuous running — a tremendous feat of physical and mental stamina (and agility for the lap counters), often winning the race himself. Hart House has enthusiastically supported the Run for the ROM. In 1995, it inaugurated the popular Hart House Triathlon. The north wing remains a centre for judo, karate, and other combative sports.

But it is the focus upon inclusive fitness, instruction, and unstructured recreation that gives Hart House athletics such vibrant relevance today. The handsome 1992 renovations of the locker rooms, which finally created equal dressing rooms for women and men, both with direct access to the pool, consolidated the transformation. The north wing continues to engage thousands of students and others in vigorous physical activity, and introduce them to new activities and skills, many of which will serve for a lifetime. Whether it helps them to gain a fuller sense of self, to make and strengthen friendships or simply to reduce stress, it continues to encourage them in a life of disciplined thought and exertion. Through its proximity to the intellectual and cultural activities of the south wing, it continues to link the cultures of the body to those of the mind and spirit. In all these ways, it complements, and enriches in wondrous ways, a university education. Amateurism, the variant of athletic masculinity traditionally championed by Hart House, which stressed intellect, public service, civility, and culture along with athletic prowess, is worth preserving, if in an updated, more inclusive form.

Despite the dramatic change in purpose, activities, and demographics, I suspect the old amateur patriarchs would approve.

The Hart House Track today

The entrance to the Farm

Chapter 9
The Farm

Klara Michal

Just an hour's journey from Toronto, you can sit on the ridge of the Niagara Escarpment and scan the panoramic view of a beautiful landscape. Students and staff of the University of Toronto have been enjoying this view since 1949, when Hart House Farm was purchased for $8,500 by Warden Nicholas Ignatieff in order to enable the students to "strike a reasonable balance between urban pursuits and country activities, a worthy object of broader education." As a result of this vision, the 150-acre property has blossomed into a wonderful escape that has been enjoyed by more than 200,000 people over the last 50 years.

At the time of the purchase, two farmhouses stood on the land — Snyder House and Ignatieff House. Walter Snyder, who sold the property to Hart House, was a great friend of the students and agreed to stay on to oversee the property. Leading a very spartan existence in his home, Snyder was "like a living history book," according to Gordon West, current chair of the Farm Committee, which runs the farm along with staff from Hart House.

Back in the early days, a small group of undergraduate students, West among them, administered and worked on the farm, bringing in electricity and plumbing, and making it accessible to large groups of students. The barn that sits beside Ignatieff House was built by Eric Andersen, the first farm resident after Snyder's death in 1952. Later on, in the 1970s, with the help of Finnish Exchange students, Hart House staff built the sauna using the farm's own cedar. To this day the sauna remains a highlight of any trip up to the farm. More recently, a sweat lodge was built on the edge of a pond. It was later moved up to sit on the crest of a hill.

With time the farm has ceased to be solely a place for relaxation — special events, conferences, seminars, and even weddings regularly take place there.

Gordon and Heather Warn, the current residents, tend to the farm and help oversee the many work days the Committee organizes throughout the year to maintain the land — planting, clearing, and much more.

Washing dishes, *c.*1970

A bonfire by the pond

130

The farm traditionally hosts four major events every year, one for each season. The rich crimsons and golds of the maple leaves lure people up to work the old-fashioned cider press for "Cider 'n' Song." It is hoped that the orchard planted for the farm's fortieth anniversary will soon begin supplying the apples used to make the cider.

Cross-country skiing, skating, and making snow creatures are highlights of the "Winter Carnival." This January event draws people to see the crisp, clean snow blanketing the farm and to savour hot chocolate and a warm fire. The sauna is usually on full steam for those brave enough to jump through a hole in the ice covering the pond.

Sawing off

At this time of year, visitors and staff alike help saw and split about twelve cords of wood, which is then loaded onto trucks and hauled down to fuel the fireplaces of Hart House.

In March, as the days grow warmer, the sap begins flowing, and we hold our spring event, "Sugaring Off." The farm's new evaporator can boil down two hundred gallons of sap per hour, which sounds like a lot, but it isn't actually so much when you consider that between forty and fifty gallons of sap are required to make one gallon of syrup. A whole day spent gorging on toffee, sweet syrup, and pancakes makes this the most delicious event of the year at the farm. The syrup—the pride and joy of the farm—is bottled and sold throughout the year at the Porters' Desk in Hart House, where it is also used in the Gallery Grill.

The farm is teeming with wildlife, and in the spring, while hiking around the property, you can see deer, foxes, coyotes, and eastern bluebirds.

Our summer event, "Midsummer Night's Eve," consists of two full days of warmth, magic, and the odd fairy or two. For the last couple of years, a group has cycled up from Hart House on the first day, meeting those who drove or took the bus.

Both days are filled with activities—volleyball on the playing field, informal matches of catch, swimming, hiking—music, and, of course, food. Sometimes we have dug a fire pit and buried food to cook all day on the hot coals underground. One year, there was an ambitious plan to roast an entire pig. The problem was that the pig delivered was twice the size of that originally ordered and too big to turn on the spit. Eventually it had to be carved up and finished off in the oven.

Most people entering the university first hear about the farm and visit it in September. Students from the St. George, Scarborough, and Mississauga campuses come up for orientation sessions that reveal a very different side of the university. Over the years, many come back to escape the hustle and bustle of the city.

This year marks the fiftieth anniversary of the farm. Plans include planting more fruit and nut trees in the orchard, as well as other trees elsewhere to return the landscape to its original woodland state.

The future of the farm has sometimes been in doubt, but the hope is that an endowment can be established to ensure future generations a place of respite and repose, shared activities and fellowship. With the growing craziness of our world, Hart House Farm becomes more and more precious and irreplaceable.

A cast party in Warden Joseph McCulley's apartment

Chapter 10
The House as Home
Val Ross

On a Friday afternoon at Hart House, the clouds scud over the sunny quad. In the cathedral-roofed gymnasium, one of the loftiest, airiest exercise rooms in the world, men and women of diverse sizes, shapes, colours, and ages lift weights and pedal fervently on exercycles. In the Gallery Grill, alumnae in high heels and frosted hair toast the end of the week with glasses of wine at tables overlooking the stained-glass, light-splashed Great Hall. In the Library, a lone young man sleeps off a late night on a leather couch. In the Debates Room, Islamic students kneel for Friday prayers.

"Hart House has been more than wonderful," says Ms Aynur Rabbani, an activist with the Muslim Students Federation. She praises the House staff for its weekly efforts to prepare the room. "We don't have to do a thing. They installed pegs on either side of all the paintings so that they can be covered—we can have no images in our religion—and then they cover the paintings with beige muslin cloths. They move the furniture too."

With all the heavy chairs out of the way, the Debates Room—where once young men met to jeer down resolutions about the emancipation of women, where once the young John F. Kennedy, future president of the United States, debated Stephen Lewis, future leader of the Ontario New Democratic Party—is transformed with mats and carpets to accommodate as many as two hundred and fifty worshippers, men at the front and women, according to Islamic practice, at the back.

The stone neo-Gothic corridors of Hart House still echo with nostalgia for an Oxbridge past, a Rupert Brooke-ish world of idealistic young men, poetry, and privilege. But Hart House has evolved beyond that. Poised at the brink of the twenty-first century, it is no longer an unassailable citadel of Anglo-Saxon, Christian masculinity. Once its halls smelled of pipe smoke and male sweat; now it is unisex deodorant and the pong of any gender's well-used running shoes that permeate the place. Once the students solemnly agreed that ragtime was too, well,

Leaving the House after a visit in 1939, King George VI and Queen Elizabeth walk past the staff.

black to play on the House piano. On any given afternoon these days, the corridors echo with jazz and Joplin. Once high tea and boiled potatoes marked the boundaries of Hart House cuisine; now the whiff from the Arbor Room cafeteria is of Mexican chili—vegetarian, so observant Jews and Muslims, the women discreetly swathed in head coverings, can partake.

Muslims have been praying at Hart House since 1966—six years before women were allowed to enter freely, and thirteen years before the athletic facilities were fully integrated. Such profound changes in the population of the place still create small tensions and ironies.

Gay male students say they no longer feel as comfortable here as in the days when Hart House was a men's club and everyone swam nude. To overcome their discomfort, Hart House administrators feel obliged to post signs proclaiming that the House is "Positive Space," as in "gay-positive." Meanwhile non-Muslim feminists quietly fume because their Islamic sisters kneel at the back of prayer meetings and cover their heads; some argue that Hart House, in its efforts to adapt to the multicultural student population, has moved full circle back to the days when women were admitted only at restricted times to certain areas and under strict codes of behaviour.

And yet others—Muslim women such as Aynur Rabbani—say that in other ways the circle has hardly turned at all. "I am Muslim, I'm female, and I'm brown. And to me, the House is still very distinctively an Anglo-Saxon, male place," says Rabbani. "Look in the Record Room or in the Bickersteth Room. There are big dark paintings and photographs in there of white Anglo-Saxon men, looking ever so Imperial. That's still a strong flavour in the House."

No one is more aware of the contradictions within the Hart House communities than Margaret Hancock. As Hart House warden, and the first woman to hold that job, she says, "Hart House has to keep transforming itself. We have to have a cross-cultural, gender-neutral, inclusive vision." As warden, Hancock has inherited the first-floor office to the left of the guest book, whose pages bear witness to some of the House's more celebrated visitors: royalty (King George VI, Elizabeth II, the Prince of Wales, and the Duke of Edinburgh), American presidents, Canadian prime ministers.

Hancock works here, and lives in the warden's apartment on the third floor with her husband and two daughters. "It is so beautiful here, it's tempting to hunker down and not bring the world in. But we must."

She must also mediate among all the interests that claim, use, criticize, and cherish Hart House. Such delicate balancing of the interests of the two hundred student groups on campus and the forty thousand full- and part-time students is all part of Hancock's job. But the warden also deals with another community— one of which few twenty-year-olds of any gender, race, ethnic or religious background are aware: the ghosts of people who built this place and gave it a meaning in their lives, in the city, and beyond.

Vincent Massey had not yet attended Oxford when he first dreamed of a place like Hart House. Already, however, the psychological elements that would shape it—

the anglophilic elitism, the sexism, the yearning for community, the admirable Methodist desire to do good and help others on the path to self-improvement, and the genuine and ambitious love of the arts—were strong elements of his character.

In his sexism, Massey was merely a creature of his time, but he carried his commitment to gender apartheid until his death in 1967. The reasons may be locked in his childhood. In 1903, when he was sixteen, his beloved mother, Anna Vincent, died of appendicitis while she was travelling with her two sons, Vincent and Raymond, in London. Their father, Chester, could not fill the emotional void left by his wife's death. Not surprisingly, young Vincent tried to rediscover a sense of family and community in school.

He loathed Jarvis Collegiate, the co-educational public high school in Toronto where he was enrolled. In the year of his mother's death, he moved to St. Andrew's, an all-boys Methodist private college then located in Rosedale. He lived there Monday to Friday, returning to the gloomy family mansion only on weekends. Vincent must have decided that a boys' boarding school was for him; he threw himself into track and field, became first lieutenant in the cadet corps, and revelled in the prestige of his position relative to the other boys.

In The Young Vincent Massey, Claude Bissell quotes an early entry in Vincent's diary concerning a visit by the lieutenant-governor to the college to see the cadet corps join the 48th Highlanders in trooping the colours: "We officers went to the House afterwards for refreshments. The Common Soldiers ate on the lawn!" Common Soldiers, indeed—years later, Carman Guild, then assistant warden of programming at Hart House, was chatting with Bissell. Guild recalls, "One of us—and it wasn't me—said, 'You know, Vincent was a terrible snob.'"

On his twenty-first birthday, in 1908, Vincent joined his father, his uncle, and his aunt as an executor of the Massey Estate. He soon assumed an active role in several projects the executors had under way. One was a report on the colleges and secondary schools supported by the Methodist Church of Canada. Vincent chaired the committee. His report reiterated his strong belief that it is in sexually segregated boarding schools that young men are most likely to develop a sense of honour, spiritual communion with past generations of fellows, and consciousness of duty. His fellow commissioners agreed that co-education was an unsatisfactory arrangement for secondary schooling. (We have come full circle; now it is feminist educators such as Carol Gilligan who argue that separating girls from boys permits the girls a better chance to excel.)

When Vincent became an executor of the Estate he was an undergraduate at the University of Toronto. Already he was urging his uncles and aunt to consider giving the university a new men's athletic and social building, which could house the YMCA and the Student Christian Movement all under one roof; they would name it after their father, and his grandfather, Hart Massey. Vincent was so enthused he postponed pursuing his history studies at Oxford to preside over the new project. Finally, in 1911, after the first sod was turned, he left Toronto for England to take up graduate studies in history at Balliol College, Oxford. Already an anglophile, Vincent was enchanted by Oxford. What he saw and experienced among the dreaming spires, he resolved to bring home—the pleasures of beauty and art; the clubby satisfactions of quiet reading and good conversation, the assurance

Actors relax in the Arbor Room after a performance, c.1955.

The sudden death of my father, who was then warden, in the shadow of Soldiers' Tower in March 1952 was so traumatic for me that my memories of my Hart House years were walled off for a long time. But in truth they were the years I spent with Father. He had left for the war eight months before I was born, to return in 1946. We moved into the warden's apartment in the summer of 1947. It was a strange place for a young lad. Perched at the top of fifty-two steps — a long ribbon of a place, with a lovely view, through small leaded panes and the branches of tall maples, of the playing field to the west.

Sometimes Father and I got up early to kick a soccer ball around on those fields, and I remember in the afternoon joining the crowds of students on the sidelines watching inter-faculty football, occasionally dodging the flying bodies.

But my solitary playground was the roofs — slate and copper, populated by pigeons, and offering unencumbered views of the city. I can't remember exactly how I got up there — out a window somewhere. It was best that Mother didn't know.

Nicholas Ignatieff

of privilege and exclusivity. Plans for Hart House changed. And then war broke out in 1914 and construction slowed to a near-standstill.

Though the company of young men was Vincent's idea of heaven, he was a confirmed heterosexual, albeit with all the proper Victorian restraints. His diary in his early twenties records blushing encounters with young ladies. He writes that a beautiful stenographer in the Massey-Harris Co.'s office reduced him to stuttering gibberish.

In 1914 he began courting one of the great well-connected beauties of his day. She was Alice Parkin, daughter of Sir George Parkin, a Canadian who had become secretary of the Cecil Rhodes Trust, with friends in the upper ranks of the Anglican Church in England. Alice arrived in Toronto to head one of the women's residences at the university, women having been admitted to the university since 1884. She had many male admirers, but she married Vincent in 1915. She was eight years his senior—a mother figure, one suspects.

Alice Massey was, like her young husband, an anglophile, a snob, and a lover of theatre, art, and books. She joined him in his enthusiasm for the Hart House project, helping choose furnishings and fabrics, imposing her taste for strong colours and vigorous contrasts.

But she too approved of separating men and women at school and at play. Still, she herself always had access to the events she enjoyed—she served on the board of the Players' Club which used the theatre, helped choose directors, and designed costumes for productions.

When Hart House opened in 1919, the rejoicing spread well beyond campus. The Prince of Wales paid a visit and pronounced, "This reminds me so much of Oxford. You can teach us how to do things over here." The Toronto Telegram pronounced, "This unique university men's club is unduplicated on this continent and that really means in the world."

But though the House professed to be open to all, it was not. "Old photos of Hart House show returning veterans, shoulder to shoulder," says Margaret Hancock, "yet no one ever raised the question of access for the disabled." (Ramps would not be installed until the 1980s; Hancock is only now planning elevator access to upper floors.) Students in certain faculties were not allowed to join Hart House; pharmacy students were not admitted until 1929. Sensing a strong Protestant tone to the place, Catholics had to be courted with visits to St. Michael's College on the other side of Queen's Park. And, of course, the heavy doors were closed to young women except on specified, special occasions.

One of the first women to object was Marie Parkes, then secretary-treasurer of the Women's Student Advisory Council—within the decade, she would become the chaperone of the first Canadian Women's Olympic team. Parkes and a group of other women students went to the university administration to protest their exclusion from the new building. They said that the Lillian Massey's building at University and Bloor was already inadequate for the young women on campus; its swimming pool was so small, it had already been nicknamed "the bathtub."

The administration promised the women a parallel building of their own. The Women's Building Committee was struck with Parkes at the fore. The committee would wait, holding bake sales and candy sales—and holding its breath—for forty

CBC Conference

THE REAL WORLD OF WOMAN

In 1962, ten years before women were admitted as members, the CBC held this conference at Hart House.

years before the university finally kept its promise and opened the Benson Building women's athletic facility in 1960.

In the meantime, women students did not sit by and wait for Hart House to permit them to enter as members. They pushed and they pressed, and when they were beaten back, they pushed again. On March 21, 1921, the Varsity complained that the gymnasium and the tank (the swimming pool) had been used three times in the past year by women, who were admitted only because of a special arrangement with the Department of Education. The article explained that this arrangement was made only during hot summer months, and only in the early hours of the morning when men were not using the facilities.

But the privilege had encouraged presumption of privilege, the article warned.

This year the women wished to use the Hart House tank twice a month. If this were granted it would become an institution and not a special occasion ...A little reflection will convince anyone of the impracticability of conducting a single tank and gymnasium for both men and women...As Warden Bowles explained, "This is not a dog in the manger attitude but one dictated by simple expediency."

In 1921, Walter Bowles was replaced by a new warden, one who would help determine the character of Hart House and its community for decades. J. Burgon Bickersteth was in many ways an ideal warden. He was liberal and open to new ideas; he often was called upon to defend the right of the House to invite in labour and left-wing speakers for debates. His diary records that he was thrilled to have Paul Robeson, the first black graduate of Columbia's law school, join him at head table in the Great Hall, and decorously refrained from asking Robeson, who was able to only find work singing and acting, to perform for the students. (Robeson volunteered in any case and gave an impromptu concert after lunch.)

But we may certainly suspect Burgon Bickersteth guilty of sexism. You can see this in the events of the winter of 1928–29.

The Debates Committee had invited MP Agnes Macphail to come to Hart House and speak to the motion, "That in the opinion of this House the emancipation of women has not lived up to its early promise."

The invitation caused quite a flap among many of the young males on campus. Early in January, one wrote to the *Varsity*. It is worth reprinting this letter in full because it suggests so much about the peculiar combination of anglophilic nostalgia and genial male chauvinism in the Hart House community at the time.

Editor, The Varsity —

Dear Sir:
Your latest issue confirms the rumour that when Miss Agnes Macphail, M.P., will speak on the failure of women's emancipation at the next Hart House debate, Wednesday, January 23, some representative women undergraduates will be present in the gallery as spectators. Are the Rights of man to be violated without protest?

November 1957, Hart House: outside, a spirited band of women picketed and protested their exclusion. Snugly within, John F. Kennedy and his all-male audience allowed themselves a moment of mutual satisfaction. Said the future president: "It is a pleasure to be in a country where [women] cannot mix in everywhere."

It was distinctly not a pleasure to be on the receiving end of such contempt. It was a shock, on my arrival on campus the next year, to learn I was barred from Hart House: as a child actress, I'd performed there often and felt a privileged attachment to its theatre.

The sting of discrimination was particularly sharp on cold winter nights when I whiled away the hours after class, awaiting some evening lecture or concert, in the only public space available — the bleakly fluorescent-lit library. I pictured the men lolling in their easy chairs, reading or listening to music while the fire crackled on the hearth.

If I'd known then of Kennedy's comment, I would not have been surprised. Male supremacy was the air we breathed; we took it into ourselves as silently and destructively as inhaling asbestos. Most of the students who studied English at University College never noticed or questioned the fact that all our professors were male. No one challenged the fact that the future Massey College was to be all-male. When I visited the then-dean of women at my college to protest the segregation at Hart House, her frosty disdain made me feel that my indignation was bizarre, if not deviant.

The closed face of Hart House was a daily reminder that the university itself deemed us women to be somehow substandard — tolerated, on sufferance, but certainly not equal. The harm was subtle, but it was more than symbolic.

Michele Landsberg

Rather than a single memory, Hart House to me was a backdrop to life at the University of Toronto in the 1970s. But it was a very large and distinctive backdrop.

Its benefectors had clearly intended Hart House to have the air of a dignified, Oxonian, upper-class men's club. With its neo-Gothic structure, imposing Great Hall, rooms with large fireplaces and padded leather chairs—and the exclusion of women—it was a place likely to suit the tastes of any Oxford don. One could certainly imagine sherry being served in the Bickersteth Room after a debate about the military accomplishments of the Boer War.

All this fit fairly well with a certain element at the university—the elitist, private-schoolish, Upper Canadian atmosphere that could be found in concentrated doses, for instance, at Trinity College.

But by the early 1970s, the intentions of the Hart House benefactors had been subverted, or at least partly subverted, due to pressure from a student body with little taste for keeping alive the spirit of the old order.

Scenes that would have alarmed the most liberal Oxford don became common—people in clothes that were not just casual but actually scruffy could be seen eating in the Great Hall next to clutches of tweed-jacketed professors with unnecessary patches at the elbow. Worse still, there were now women walking freely in the halls, even sprawling on the leather chairs or moving their limbs in the athletic wing.

Hart House had definitely changed. The Oxford pretension was still there, but it had been forced to mix with a kind of down-home egalitarianism that had a distinctly Canadian flavour. One could say that Hart House had been, if not fully liberated from its upper-class roots, at least forced to accommodate a more popular culture. In a sense, it had been Canadianized.

Linda McQuaig

Last year the men of University College debated with the co-eds over the outrageous proposal (as are all such proposals) that the institution of afternoon tea in one of the common rooms of Hart House for members and the so-called 'fairer sex' would enhance the gracious amenities of our university life. It was then wisely decided that it would do nothing of the kind. With a becoming and exemplary modesty the women themselves opposed their own entrance to the male Holy of Holies. I would commend this attitude to the women of 1929. They have forgotten their place ... The ravages of feminism in our debating circles have already been notorious this season. First the present Speaker of the House was forcibly and mysteriously carried away from this citadel of manhood and celibacy [presumably he left to get married]. Now his predecessor, bewitched, wavers on the verge of marriage. I cannot continue this painful recital. It is the beginning of the end. Let it suffice that we must band together to resist this invasion, and protect our undergraduates; to be on guard in case they should even capture our Warden and so make off with the very heart of Hart House.

By admitting women the committee is guilty of prejudicing the question before it is decided. Let Miss Macphail come—as usual, some devil's advocate must be among us ... But women as spectators (a contradiction in terms anyway)—never! What will happen to the decorum of the House, the ties, the clothes, the talk, the attitudes struck; what will happen to the robust manly stories of unblushing and two-fisted derring-do. Perhaps all will be mistakenly decorous and ladylike; perhaps, and this is more to this female generation's taste, all will be wholly irrational, excited, personal, unparliamentary and illogical. One thing is sure, it will not be a real Hart House Debate. Be prepared sir, lest strenuous amazons storming the gates of our last refuge and sanctuary will have it fall to their wiles, lest Hart House for men, by men and of men will perish off the face of this saddened earth.

The letter is signed "L.M.G." Almost assuredly this was the young Lionel Morris Gelber, one of the few Jews then active in Hart House (in both debating and drama) and soon to be Canada's first Jewish Rhodes scholar. Gelber's family laughed aloud when I read them the letter. "He was just taking a position for the sake of it! He was a progressive thinker," they chortled. And indeed, Gelber was soon to be a strong advocate for the drafting of women into the Canadian armed services. But it says much about Hart House—and the arch, masculine, Oxonian tone maintained under Bickersteth—that a voice such as L.M.G.'s would be heard.

The *Varsity* printed a response in the next issue. "Dear Sir—I agree that Hart House is essentially for men, and that its fast disappearing tradition should be tenaciously clung to," the female author wrote. But she added plaintively that women would not be pressing to attend debates at Hart House or use its athletic facilities if they had an option: "As long as we have no refuge of our own we will be curious. How many men contributed to our mile of nickels? How many bought candy on Monday? Please give us a hand with our building fund even if it is just to get rid of us ... "

Summer students in the quadrangle, 1968

Warden Margaret Hancock (right) mixes with students at
Wide Open House.

In any case, when Macphail came to speak, forty women were admitted to the Debates Room, but only as spectators. They were restricted to the gallery and watched as the men defeated the motion that the emancipation of women was a disappointment by 127 votes to 71. It was a silly motion anyway, poorly worded, one that would permit agreement between a rabid feminist (who would take the position that women had not been able to get far enough) and a rabid misogynist (who would argue that women were incapable of living up to any early promise). The *Varsity* reported that "Miss Macphail gave a forceful address to great applause and much laughter."

In my final undergraduate year, 1971–1972, I applied to Miss Bolitho for a job in food services. My eventual assignment was in the Gallery Club, Monday night shift. Gertie Duncan was in charge, greeting the (always) male diners at the door and checking the Book to make sure they were in fact members.

But as Warden Bickersteth recalled it for Ian Montagnes, "Once, and only once, we invited a woman as visitor—Agnes Macphail, and we asked her because she was then the only woman member of Parliament...I was disappointed in the standard of speaking." Whether it was Macphail's speaking or that of the men who refused to take her seriously, he didn't say.

Despite such attitudes, women continued to press for admission to Hart House and to make guerrilla forays. The *Varsity* records one incident in October 1929, the week the U.S. stock market collapsed and plunged the world into recession: "two pretty co-eds" entered the House and demanded a shoeshine from Mr. Wilson in the barbershop. "You shouldn't be here," he pleaded. "The locker rooms and showers are too adjacent." One invader retorted, "They shouldn't be here then." A moustached staff member was called to lead them out. Mr. Wilson later told the *Varsity*: "They must have been freshettes doing an initiation stunt. Downright rudeness would have been necessary to get rid of them so I let one have her shoeshine."

A big bonus of working as a waitress at Hart House was that you got fed first. The food was substantial and all the staff took one look at my thin frame and urged me to eat, eat, eat.

My uniform was a black French-maid affair with white cuffs and collar that the seasoned hands helped me pin on down in the locker room below stairs. Here was my first exposure to the world of working women and their own brand of locker-room talk—about the cook's helper who had to leave her unemployed husband carfare every day so he could look for a job, about another Gallery Club waitress (Tuesday nights) who put on airs, about the professor at the high table last week who had the nerve to ask Nellie to peel his banana.

Women pursued serious avenues too. Throughout the 1920s, there was no sign of the promised athletic facility of their own. By the middle of the 1930s, some Hart House stewards were starting to agree that the situation was unjust, or at least socially awkward. They approached Vincent Massey to bend the rules and make the House more accessible to female undergraduates. In February 1937, Massey replied, writing the rebels a stern letter:

Sometimes I was called to serve at a banquet—a financial windfall because I was guaranteed three hours of work at the princely sum of $2.50 per hour, as opposed to $1.70 in the Gallery Club.

> I write to you stating clearly the views of the Founders of Hart House as regards the question of women...the building shall be for the men of the university and not for the women...The Great Hall was planned for the use of men only...equipment exists for the use of the men...I should have thought that all these points would be generally understood by now... Where it was thought necessary an interpretation has been quite liberal as regards the admission of women to certain events, such as a limited number of dances, the Sunday evening concerts and the Monthly Visitors days.

One night, after a huge and rowdy banquet, I was getting ready to clock out when a supervisor asked me to serve a meal to the band, newly arrived for their after-dinner gig. Royally miffed as I was at the extra work and practically flinging the food on the table, imagine my humiliation when the band leader called me over and presented me with $2.00 for my efforts.

And that was that.

Burgon Bickersteth retired in 1947. His successor was Nicholas Ignatieff, a bona fide aristocrat—descendant of csarist nobility—and also a family man. Ignatieff moved his wife and son into the House, but because Hart House was a men-only building, Helen Ignatieff was obliged to use the back stairs to get to the family apartment on the third floor.

Susan Helwig

The Ignatieffs brought in a new and more liberal spirit, but as long as Vincent Massey was alive, nothing could change. And as things turned out, Ignatieff died suddenly in 1952 and was replaced by Joseph McCulley. Despite his liberal views, he too was unable to effect real change, or to challenge the will of the founder.

The few women who lived or worked at Hart House had to negotiate carefully around its all-male policy. Audrey Hozack, a young war widow, started work as a secretary at the Students' Administrative Council, then headquartered in Hart House, on the same day that Warden Ignatieff began his term.

Hozack soon learned that she would have to leave the building and dash over to University College in order to use a toilet. There wasn't one for women until the 1950s — and then, as she remembers it, it was "in the basement under the Great Hall in a room that is now a utility cupboard." Women were not allowed to use the Tuck Shop. There was no place to eat, so female staff were given an extra fifteen minutes at lunch hour in order to sprint to a local diner. Hozack also remembers having to wear a hat, stockings, and gloves, "and to walk on the north side of the corridors only, without speaking to the young men."

For all that it was a forbidding place for women, however, Hozack recalls it as remarkably open in other senses. "I remember walking across campus one day with one young man who was very dark-skinned, from India. People told me it was not appropriate to walk with him. Yet my friend had had no trouble at all at Hart House."

Within the grey stone walls, Hart House provided community for lonely young men, and gently eased them like stray threads into the fabric of campus life. Writing in *Saturday Night* magazine in 1978, Morris Wolfe recalled being a young working-class Jew arriving at Hart House in the late 1950s. "I was too frightened of others to attend classes often, and I compiled a dismal academic record. But I did begin to get an education...at Hart House," he wrote.

> I spent hours in the magazine room reading the best British, American and Canadian journals. In the Library I devoured countless books that were on no required lists; in the Record Room I heard much of the basic classical repertoire for the first time...Everywhere in the building hung the best Canadian art. Hart House opened windows for me...

And Hart House was one of several discreet sanctuaries for students who were gay. Brian Pronger, now a professor in the university's athletics department, has written in The *Arena of Masculinity* of the special codes of cruising and consummating in the locker room at Hart House. "To others, the gay activity was not obvious, ever," Audrey Hozack remembers. "But Warden Joe McCulley was a genial host and entertained many of the members in his apartment. There were some objections from parents. Many of these young men took good care of Joe when he was ill in later years." But more than cruising, of course, the House provided a safe environment in which gay members and staff could flourish and make significant contributions.

In the 1950s and early 1960s, wardens Ignatieff and McCulley quietly tried to liberalize Hart House's restrictions on women. They were admitted to a meeting of the Library Committee in 1953 to hear Marshall McLuhan, professor of English at St Michael's College, speak on the study of communications and his new book, *The Mechanical Bride*. They were admitted to the art gallery and to music recitals on Wednesday afternoons. They were to be allowed to eat in the Great Hall on special occasions ("Babes welcome at Hart House Invitation Dinner," proclaimed the *Varsity* on January 19, 1956). Under Warden McCulley, the Arbor Room in the basement welcomed women, though only after lunch hour. But the basic rule remained in place.

Linda Silver Dranoff arrived on campus in 1957 with a strong sense of justice (not surprisingly, she later became a lawyer and judge). She recalls her anger when she learned that women would not be permitted to attend the Hart House debate between a young American senator, John F. Kennedy, and Stephen Lewis, son of one of the founders of the NDP. She and several other angry young women went to petition the warden.

"We said, 'Please, Warden McCulley, let us in to hear the next president of the United States.' I remember his bemused smile," Silver Dranoff recalls. "We thought if we were reasonable and not extreme we might get somewhere. He told us, 'My hands are tied.' I do remember how bemused he was at the children coming to beg."

Though turned away, the children returned with a vengeance. On the cold, rainy November night of the debate, Silver Dranoff joined a lusty picket line under the open windows of the Debates Room. "We marched with our umbrellas, up and down. We chanted, I don't remember what. We kept it up until the end." Later, both Stephen Lewis and John Kennedy sent the women students their apologies.

When Joe McCulley retired in 1965, and Arnold Wilkinson took over, Hart House was still a men's club. Meanwhile, more women were coming into the building, women such as Dorothy Thomas, secretary to the Hart House Orchestra under Boyd Neel.

"Outside of the female staff," Thomas recalls, "I was the only woman who could come and go. I loved it. I was not enlightened in those days. Can you imagine just being able to swan in?" She laughs aloud. "I liked the exclusivity, the special position. It had a wonderful clubby atmosphere. And there was a thrill of going into a place so lovely. The Library was enchanting. Coming from an immigrant working-class family as I did, Hart House opened up the world for me, a romantic English heritage ... Did I want other women there?" Thomas laughs. "I did not!" Still, she cheered when a woman friend, dressed as a boy, crashed a Hart House debate. "Outrage!" she laughs again.

Finally, in 1967, the old man with the strong sexual segregationist views died of pneumonia, in London, England, surrounded by flowers sent by the Queen Mother.

"Vincent was very keen on ladies," says Carman Guild. "He was dead keen on Alice, the sun rose and set on Alice. But he was of the same mind when he was put in his coffin: education for gentlemen was best carried on by gentlemen among gentlemen." Still, at the news of his death, some women cheered.

Warden Wilkinson began preparing for the inevitable admission of women to Hart House. The first woman, a student named Vicky Little, was elected to the

Board of Stewards. The board broached the subject with the Massey Foundation. Hart House consulted lawyers about the very clear terms of the deed of gift. In 1971, Carman Guild began writing a report for the Presidential Advisory Committee on the Future Role of Hart House, recommending the admission of women. "In 1971 there is wide agreement that there can be no real sense of membership in an academic family which does not take into account the co-educational nature of that family," the document states.

Meanwhile, women students were no longer as forgiving as they had been about the anachronism of a student facility that excluded 40 to 50 percent of the student population. The Student Council declared itself fully behind the women. Michael Ignatieff, nephew of the late warden, and a member of the Debates Committee, warned of a "state of war" between women and the House. Other male students, such as David Keeble, tried to resign their membership and automatic dues paid to Hart House to protest its no-women policy.

Yet even while the deed of gift was being changed, Hart House staff continued to enforce the old rules. In 1971, an undergraduate named Liz Stewart attempted to use the Library—appropriately enough, to read Germaine Greer's article in *Esquire* on that defiant sexist, Norman Mailer. Two staff members ejected Stewart, who swore at them. Women's patience had vanished.

Abby Hoffman, one of Canada's top runners and an Olympic medallist, was also ejected when she tried to use the Hart House track to train. (Hoffman was an old hand at this; she had also been thrown out for trying to use the track for winter training in the mid-1960s.)

The House invited all members to a series of meetings to give them an opportunity to air their views. "Many of the senior members really did not want women," recalls Hozack. At an open meeting, Rosalind Stone, a professor in the athletics department, asked precisely what it was that men found so difficult about letting women in. After a silence, an older gentleman admitted that for years he had treasured being able to come to a place where he could swim in the nude. The professor agreed warmly. "Fine, we'll swim without bathing suits too." The meeting dissolved into laughter.

And then, late in 1971, word came: the deed of gift would be changed. The Massey Foundation agreed that women should be admitted to Hart House.

Warden Wilkinson telephoned Audrey Hozack, who had left to work for the Alumni Association, to ask if she would agree to become the first woman assistant warden. She had to be interviewed for the position by two vice-presidents of the university, one of whom told her, "I don't think you're ready." An hour later he telephoned and apologized. "That was stupid. The job is yours."

At first it was not easy. The House manager refused to take orders from a woman. So did the accountant. And other female secretaries were "quite resentful," she remembers; one even refused to type her letters. Even the beautiful building itself was not fully welcoming. "The stairs are very broad," says Hozack. "They are designed for men, not for women."

On the first day of term in 1972, the Hart House doors opened to admit women students. Assistant Warden Hozack stood in the front hall, beaming with triumph, to greet them. "I said, 'Welcome to Hart House!' and they looked at me strangely,"

The class with which I didn't graduate from U of T—"5T7"—was a vintage group, as I remember, including future achievers who ranged in political convictions from Stephen Lewis to Ted Rogers and in interest and future fame from the sciences to poetry to the law.

I had an excuse for not finishing my studies. I was editor of the Varsity, *heir to a long tradition of running the paper instead of going to classes and writing editorials rather than essays.*

The Varsity *in those days was run out of the basement of the old university observatory, a pencil's toss from Hart House, and an easy walk for everything from morning coffee to a moment's solitude in the middle of a busy editorial day. It was a haven of civility and friendship, even if, alas, so much of it was male. Lunch—sometimes even dinner—was a chance to absorb not only the sustenance of the Great Hall's cafeteria but the wisdom of the* Areopagitica *on its walls, which, of course, we admired somewhat more than we memorized. And the reading rooms, the debates rooms, all the various nooks and crannies with their leather armchairs and their air of tranquility, even the gym from time to time, all provided*

Hozack recalls. "To me this was the Big Day. To them, they had been coming in so gradually, it didn't mean as much."

Before long, however, she realized that it meant a lot to some. An alumna of the 1920s made the trip from Stratford, Ontario, to stay overnight in one of the guest rooms when she found that it was possible. She told Hozack how, as an architecture student, she had been obliged to sit outside the building on a camp stool sketching the exterior of Hart House while her male fellow students went in to draw.

It took another seven years to complete renovations in the basement and open up women's locker rooms that would make the athletic facilities fully integrated. Abby Hoffman presided when the Hart House women's athletic facilities opened in 1979.

———

On the brink of a new millennium, Hart House is used by dozens of campus groups. Though Hindu students have just decided to discontinue use of the chapel for weekly Pooja, they hold their annual Diwali festivities at Hart House. Once the House considered itself non-denominational because it accommodated both Baptist and Catholic Christians. Today Wiccans and Pagans (two separate groups) hold their weekly worship meetings in the Bickersteth Room.

Political access has always been a field of contention. It still is. In the fall of 1998, a member of the Conservative provincial government—highly unpopular in campus circles—rented the Great Hall for a political fundraising event. Students picketed the House, and one of the student members of the Board of Stewards brought a motion that Hart House should not be used for such political events.

"I was really pleased," says Warden Margaret Hancock. "This let us discuss freedom of expression. Senior members of the House were the staunchest defenders. This was a moment of conveying values from one generation to the next."

In trying to assure all communities on campus—cultural, religious, ethnic—that the House is a home for them, Hancock has found herself in yet another conundrum. One person's inclusion can be another's exclusion, real or perceived. "Now we put up posters in the Positive Space campaign to assure gay people that they're welcome." After her staff put up posters, "That started a debate. People said to me, 'The House is open to everyone, so why do we need to say so?' But doors can only be opened by people who perceive that they can be opened. Hart House must continue to say welcome in as many ways as it can."

an all-too-rare glimpse into what those of us burrowing away in our journalistic catacombs were missing in our single-mindedness: books, conversation, and a chance to reflect and grow.

I'm sure Joe knew all this. Joe, of course, was Joe McCulley, who was famous among us for his apparent ability to remember the name of everyone—or certainly every male undergraduate—he'd ever met. Joe knew what we were getting from Hart House: refuge, respite, and, in an even-then bewildering campus, a place to belong. He was interested in us, or so he led us to believe (which was all that mattered), and the constant twinkle in his eye as he inquired as to our welfare let us know—or realize now, looking back—that he understood what Stephen Leacock had acknowledged long before him, albeit from another campus: that the true value of a university lies in a thousand places, not all of them, or at least not all of them called, classrooms.

Peter Gzowski

About the Authors

Jim Bartley is a playwright, literary journalist, U of T alumnus (Vic 7T5), and somtime actor who first trod the boards at Hart House Theatre. His most recent play, *Stephen and Mr. Wilde,* was published in 1994 and has been produced across Canada. Bartley lives in Toronto and is a contributing reviewer and books columnist for the *Globe and Mail.*

John Duffy is a principal of StrategyCorp Inc., a Toronto public affairs consultancy, and a frequent media commentator on Canadian politics. A 1986 graduate, he was an active member of the Hart House Debates Committee. In 1983, Duffy won the national debating championship and the world English-language public speaking competition.

While an undergraduate at U of T, Bruce Kidd won the six miles event at the 1962 British Empire and Commonwealth Games and competed in the 1964 Olympics. Canadian Press voted him Canada's Male Athlete of the Year in 1961 and 1962. He began teaching at U of T in 1970 and is currently dean of the Faculty of Physical Education and Health.

Dr. Bruce Meyer is founder and Director of the Creative Writing Program at U of T's School of Continuing Studies, where he also teaches. He is author of fourteen books including *The Presence* and the forthcoming *The One Story: Literature and the Great Books.* A frequent broadcaster on CBC Radio, he is a former instructor in English at Trinity College and is currently faculty advisor to the Hart House Library Committee.

Klara Michal is a third year student in psychology and cognitive sciences at U of T. On full scholarship as a Canadian Merit Scholarship National Scholar,

Klara is active in numerous clubs and committees. Some of her favourite weekends are spent cooking for the hundreds of people who come out to the seasonal events at the Hart House Farm.

Ian Montagnes, a publishing consultant specializing in international development, is the former editor-in-chief of the University of Toronto Press. He has served on several committees of Hart House and is the author of the previous history of the House, *An Uncommon Fellowship* (1969).

A professional actor since 1969, Richard Partington is currently a doctoral student in theatre history at U of T's Graduate Centre for Study of Drama. He has published articles on Toronto's Jupiter Theatre (1951–4) and Italian baroque opera. His doctoral thesis explores Toronto's Crest Theatre, whose founders emerged from Hart House Theatre in the era of Robert Gill's directorship.

Brian Pronger (Trinity 8T0) served on the Hart House Music Committee in the mid-1970s and was secretary for two years in the early 1980s. He is now assistant professor of philosophy at U of T's Faculty of Physical Education and Health. He is the author of *The Arena of Masculinity: Sports, Homosexuality and the Meaning of Sex,* and his new book, *Body Fascism: Salvation and the Technology of Physical Fitness,* will be published soon.

Val Ross (UC 7T4) is a National Newspaper Award-winning arts reporter for the *Globe and Mail.* A former CBC TV researcher, she moved to *Maclean's,* where she was senior writer and then entertainment editor.

Paul Gary Russell is a Toronto writer, painter, and producer for film and television. The holder of an MA in art history (1965) with emphasis on early-twentieth-century architecture, he has served on the Hart House Art Committee, then as gallery curator, keeper of the prints and librarian, and now as a member of the Graduate Committee.

Dr. Rupert Schieder has made an enormous contribution to the University of Toronto, not only as a teacher and scholar at Trinity College, but also through his involvement in Hart House. He served on its Music Committee, first as a student in 1934 and then later as faculty advisor and chairman from 1970 until 1990. The Hart House Sunday Concert Series, owing to his dedication, is the longest-running concert series in Toronto. Each year, a Sunday concert, bearing his name, features the talents of young musicians.

Catherine D. Siddall wrote her master's thesis for U of T's Museum Studies on the art collection of Hart House. A long-time professional curator, she is also a landscape designer practicing "guerrilla gardening". She is also currently the graduate representative to the Hart House Art Committee.

About the Photographer of the Portfolio
Steven Evans holds a BAA and MA in photography and has taught and lectured
at Ryerson Polytechnic University. His work has been widely exhibited and
published throughout Canada, the U.S., and Europe and can be found in public,
private, and corporate collections around the world. His numerous honours
include two Gold National Magazine Awards.

About the Editor
A graduate of the University of Toronto and former denizen of Hart House,
David Kilgour is a Toronto-based editorial consultant and writer. [He estimates
that this project has taken ten years off his life.]

Acknowledgements

Putting together a book such as this is a massive undertaking that requires the knowledge and talents of a large number of people from diverse backgrounds. I would like to take this opportunity to mention by name some of the people who worked diligently behind the scenes to make this book a reality. To them I would like to express my gratitude for all that they contributed. Sincere thanks to the members of the Publication Committee who gave so much of their time to the project: Agnes Cserhati, Patricia Grant, Tracey Halford, Margaret Hancock, Jane Kay, Duncan MacLellan, John Parry, and Paul Gary Russell.

I would like to express our appreciation to the authors and to those who contributed memories, whose enthusiasm for the project is reflected in their writing.

The task of preparing each chapter was a daunting one, with too much information available rather than too little. I would like to thank researcher Reuven Ashtar, along with Harold Averill at the University of Toronto Archives and Scott James at the Arts and Letters Club, for finding information and putting it in some order for the writers. Also, I express our appreciation to Audrey Hozack and Vincent Tovell, who cast their experienced eyes over the manuscript and gave us valuable comments and advice.

Photographer Steven Evans devoted much time and great care to taking the signature photographs and the portfolio. His unerring eye has captured, and we are all richer for his endeavours, the beauty of Hart House. I would like to thank the entire staff of Hart House and the Hart House Theatre for their support of this project. In particular, I would like to mention the following members who went out of their way to accommodate our demands in their busy schedules: Christine Campbell, Dave Cook, Myra Emsley, Nigel Faulkner, Sam Harris, Patrick Mullen, Helen Reilly, and Judith Steiner. For their help with his chapter about the theatre, Richard Partington is grateful to Jan Bessey, Fred Euringer, David Gardner, Jack Gray, Charmion King, Eric House, Martin Hunter, Leon Major, Martha Mann,

Luella Massey, Anna Migliarisi, Lee Ramsay, Desmond Scott, Robert B. Scott, Ann Stuart, Ross Stuart, and Paul Templin. Bruce Mau, Chris Pommer, and Chris Rowat at Bruce Mau Design did a superb job of designing the book, and Bill Harnum at the University of Toronto Press was a great supporter from the beginning. Finally, I must pay tribute to David Kilgour for his invaluable contribution to the production of our text. Far from doing a simple editing job, he involved himself totally, with exceptional generosity. His broad knowledge, his intuition, and his sense of humour guided us novices unerringly.

Judi Schwartz
Chairperson, Publication Project

Index

Photographs are indicated by italic numbers.

Photograph Credits

Every effort has been made to ascertain the identities of the photographers whose images appear within these pages, but many remain unknown. Those who can be credited are: Christine Campbell: 112, 142 Arthur Chetwynd: 114–15 Steven Evans: front and back covers and endpapers, 1 (opposite), 18–19, 31–46 K.B. Jackson: p.12 Karsh of Ottawa (by special permission): 15 Robert Lansdale: 55, 61–2, 70, 71, 72, 78, 142 (copyright © the University of Toronto Archives) J. Marshall: 66 Judi Schwartz: 59 Liam Sharp: p. 126–7 University News Bureau: 139

Publication of this book was made possible with the generous support of the Government of Canada's Millennium Partnership Program.

A note on the type

This book is set in Sabon, a typeface designed by Jan Tschichold. Sabon was designed in 1966 to meet a seemingly impossible requirement: that it compose perfectly on both Monotype and Linotype typesetting equipment, each using a completely different approach to composition. The resulting face's understated elegance belies the complexity of the task and the enormity of Tschichold's accomplishment.